# Her Denali Solo

A WOMAN ALONE ON NORTH AMERICA'S HIGHEST PEAK

## Chris Lundgren

Kenmore, WA

Published by Epicenter Press

Epicenter Press
6524 NE 181st St. Suite 2
Kenmore, WA 98028.
www.Epicenterpress.com
www.Coffeetownpress.com
www.Camelpress.com

For more information go to: www.epicenterpress.com

www.chrislundgrenbooks.com

All rights reserved. No part of this book may be reproduced or transmitted in any form or by any means, electronic or mechanical, including photocopying, recording, or any information storage and retrieval system, without permission in writing from the publisher.

No generative AI was used in the conceptualization, planning, drafting, or creative writing of this work. No permission is given for the use of this material for AI training purposes.

Front cover and p. 150: © 1987 Norma Jean climbing up a crevasse at Matanuska Glacier by Clark Saunders

Photos of Norma Jean leaping a crevasse in the Matanuska Glacier, © 1987 on p. 151 and Norma Jean walking upward with skis in Hatcher Pass © 1989 on p. 149 also by Clark Saunders.

All other photos from the private collection of Norma Jean Bowers, used by permission.

Sincere thanks to Mr. Whitekeys for kindly granting permission to print the lyrics from his song, "Norma Jean," © 1986.

Her Denali Solo: A Woman Alone on North America's Highest Peak
Copyright © 2026 by Chris Lundgren

ISBN: 9781684922758 (trade paper)
ISBN: 9781684922765 (ebook)

LCCN 2025942364

# Dedication

Norma Jean:
For Dave Bowers, who's made my life one continuous adventure


Chris:
For Carl, Eric, and Perry

# Table Of Contents

Acknowledgments ..................................................... vii

Denali Climbing 101: A Few Things to
Know Before You Read This Book ........................ 1

Introduction: A Singular Tale ................................. 3

Chapter 1: Early Ambitions ..................................... 5

Chapter 2: First Expedition ..................................... 8

Chapter 3: Mt. Dan Beard ..................................... 19

Chapter 4: A Tragic End ........................................ 29

Chapter 5: A Failure of Group Dynamics ........... 35

Chapter 6: Sharpening Skills ................................ 50

Chapter 7: Team of One......................................... 54

Chapter 8: A Hair's Breadth .................................. 64

Chapter 9: Greater Heights ................................... 72

Chapter 10: Rascals ................................................ 77

Chapter 11: A Triumph of Group Dynamics ..... 81

Chapter 12: Culture Clash .................................... 87

Chapter 13: Team of One—The Sequel .............. 96

Chapter 14: Heavy Load ..................................... 102

Chapter 15: Taking Her Place at the Top .......... 107

Chapter 16: Change in Course ........................... 113

Chapter 17: Ready to Fly ................................... 119

Epilogue: Permanent Landing ......................... 125

Afterword: How This Book Came To Be .......... 128

Appendix 1: Norma Jean's 1990 Denali
Packing List ....................................................... 132

Appendix 2: Recognition from The Alaska
State Legislature ................................................ 135

Historical Notes ................................................ 136

Author's Notes ................................................... 142

Bibliography and Sources ................................. 144

About the Author .............................................. 148

Photos ................................................................ 149

# Acknowledgments

*Norma Jean*

The first people I would like to acknowledge would be Diane and Harry Johnson. They opened Wilderness Bound (outdoor education camp for kids) in the late 1970s. They taught me and trained me to be comfortable in the outdoors, climbing and hiking in the Talkeetna Range. That was the true beginning of my lifelong love of the mountains.

I would like to honor Dave Johnston (a living legend) and Dave Staeheli and Clark Saunders for encouraging me and believing I had the skills to attempt a solo. All of them strongly advised me to use a self-rescue device while on the glacier. Borrowing Dave Johnston's Bridgit device gave ideas to Dave Staeheli on how a ladder system might be better. Clark Saunders helped me rig (getting it to correctly hang from my harness and waist belt) my crevasse rescue device, and helped me paint ravens on my wands and the ladder.

Another top person would be Kevin House, who was manager at REI Anchorage while I worked there over the years. The corporate structure at the time encouraged retail staff to "walk the talk." This attitude allowed me to pursue not only climbing and skiing, but paragliding and other sports. They always "took me back" when I returned from each adventure. That flexibility in work was amazing!

A special thank you to Tom and Courtenay Murphy who managed the Hatcher Pass Lodge for many years. Tom helped to create and continue avalanche safety instruction courses for AIARE. The training I took, and then taught, with AIARE helped shape my decision-making skills. And Courtenay's advice has helped shape our financial stability.

Love must go out to Dan Lucas, Bill LaRue, Keenan and Debby Retherford, Mark Gronewald and Clark Saunders, all of whom were part of the "Ski Commandos" (my friends from Palmer who instilled in me the desire for backcountry skiing and love of the mountains. They remind me still not to take yourself too seriously).

I would really like to acknowledge my husband, Dave Bowers, too. He has a strong belief in my capabilities (sometimes when maybe he should NOT) and has continued to inspire me to try new challenges. His life is also one that could be written about in books. He has led several trans-Sierra ski tours, was a helicopter ski guide, underwater diver for sunken treasure, and more.

Dave helped me sort through old notebooks and photos and journals. His patience throughout this process was remarkable. I tend to refer to his strength and stability as "good soil" in which one can grow and bloom. Although he is very proud of my solos and my past success, he is always looking toward our next adventure. In Dave's own words: "The future is where it's at, man!"

I would like to thank Chris Lundgren for listening to my stories and believing that people would find them interesting enough for a book. The process together has been extraordinary. Thank you for your commitment to this project!

### Chris

Foremost, I would like to thank Norma Jean, who so generously opened up her life to me and who was always approachable and fun to talk with. Through this book, I've gained more insight into mountain climbing than I ever expected—and, as a huge bonus, a friend.

Bryan Burns, who contacted Norma Jean on my behalf and let me know what a good human she is.

Carl Lundgren, who realized there were only three degrees of separation between Norma Jean and me and promptly contacted his old ski pal Bryan to put us in touch. As with all my writing projects, Carl served as a sounding board and a fount of ideas.

At Epicenter Press, President Phil Garrett and Executive Editor and Associate Publisher Jennifer McCord. Thanks for seeing the value in Norma Jean's story and helping us to make the book a reality.

Clark Saunders, Norma Jean's good friend and ex-husband, who was instrumental in her solo and took some amazing photos along the way. Clark is also a friend of Carl's and mine and is well known in our community as a climber, paragliding pioneer, and fat-tire bike enthusiast. Thanks for talking with me and adding context to Norma Jean's climbing life.

Roger and Pam Robinson, who talked with me early on in the project and confirmed details about Norma Jean's climbing. Roger is also the subject of a book (*Denali Ranger: A Life of Drama and Adventure on America's Tallest Peak* by Lew Freedman) and is the father of the clean climbing and leave-no-trace movements on Denali.

To my longtime friend and fellow author Stan Jones, who directed me to Phil Garrett at Epicenter Press, reviewed my proposal, and chewed over the story with me. As always, your insights proved invaluable.

Christine and Christopher Pelky, who helped orchestrate Norma Jean's "TED Talk" presentation that gave voice to her story. Christine also suggested the book's title. I look forward to meeting you both in person someday.

Thanks, Mr. Whitekeys, for writing and performing a hilarious song about Norma Jean after her first solo attempt in 1986. I appreciate your unearthing the lyrics from your (pre-computer) archive and allowing me to publish them.

Thanks to Colby Coombs, author of the essential book, *Denali's West Buttress: A Climber's Guide to Mt. McKinley's Classic Route* (and to the late Bradford Washburn, whose clear and artful photographs enhance the pages). My copy is highlighted, flagged, underlined, and dogeared.

Thanks to Steve House and Mark Postle for their YouTube tutorial on climbing Denali's West Buttress. It is packed with practical advice and detailed descriptions that led to many "aha!" moments for me.

Deep appreciation goes to Lina Kianipour, Interlibrary Loan Assistant, Anchorage Public Library, for tracking down Denali accident reports on multiple occasions. Your behind-the-scenes work allowed me to place pieces of Norma Jean's story in the correct order and time period.

# DENALI CLIMBING 101:
## A Few Things to Know Before You Read This Book

Norma Jean Bowers ascended Denali along the popular West Buttress route. The route attracted 80 to 90 percent of Denali's climbers during Norma Jean's day in the 1980s and into 1990, and the trend continues. The West Buttress is considered the easiest of the three most common paths to the summit, yet it is fraught with all the challenges one would expect of a massive mountain just 200 miles from the Arctic Circle.

Kahiltna Base Camp serves climbers using the West Buttress route, as well as the Cassin Ridge and West Rib routes. At an elevation of 7,200 feet, the camp sits on the southeast fork of Denali's Kahiltna Glacier, about 75 air miles northwest of Talkeetna. The town—itself located 115 miles north of Anchorage—is the point of departure for a majority of expeditions.

Climbers fly into Base Camp with about 120 pounds of gear. This includes their tent, sleeping bag and pads, about three weeks' worth of food and fuel, a stove, layers of clothing and outerwear, climbing equipment, and more. The gear is split between their backpack and a sled for travel on the lower portion of the mountain.

Most climbers spend their rest days and nights acclimating at four established camps along the West Buttress route. Each has more than one name, but Camp 1 (Ski Hill Camp) is at 7,800 feet; Camp 2 (11 Camp) is at 11,200 feet; Camp 3 (14 Camp or Medical Camp) is at 14,200 feet; and Camp 4 (High Camp) is at 17,200 feet.

Climbers ski or snowshoe and camp along the Kahiltna Glacier, until the going becomes too steep, around 11,000 feet;

then they bury the skis or snowshoes in a cache for the return trip. (Sleds are likewise stored between 11,000 and 14,000 feet.) They strap crampons to their climbing boots and carry an ice axe for the steeper slopes of the upper mountain. Most teams of two or more stay roped together for safety.

There is no rock climbing on Denali; it's all snow and ice.

The mountaineering season lasts from late April to mid-July. (Before late April, the temperatures are generally colder and the wind near the summit is stronger. After mid-July, snow conditions around Base Camp can be too soft and unpredictable for bush plane landings.) Alaska's nickname is, "Land of the Midnight Sun," and Denali mountaineers enjoy nearly 24 hours of daylight during these months.

The summit stands at 20,310 feet (the most up-to-date elevation, determined in 2015). Climbers do not need to carry supplemental oxygen. They must ascend the mountain in stages, camping along the way to allow their bodies to acclimate. Without this step, they risk getting altitude sickness. Other hazards include avalanches, hypothermia, frostbite, and falling into crevasses or off steep, slippery slopes. Climbers must be prepared for snowstorms with hurricane-level winds that can last for several days at a time. In clear weather, they need sun protection, as UV exposure is greater at higher altitudes.

Those taking on Denali need to be in top-notch shape, adept in mountaineering skills, and well-schooled on what to bring and how to pack it. Flexibility, resourcefulness, and resilience are keys to making the summit, while clear-headedness and patience allow those faced with roadblocks to make good decisions—and live to climb another day.

## INTRODUCTION
## A Singular Tale

Norma Jean Bowers scored the biggest mountaineering feat you've never heard of. She was the first female climber to make a documented solo summit of Denali.

In 1990, when only 50 of the thousand annual attempts were made by women, Norma Jean summited without assistance. There was no roping to another climber along the deeply crevassed Kahiltna Glacier; no help with keeping her tent from collapsing during multi-day storms; and no clipping into fixed lines that others used on the steepest sections of the West Buttress route. Worst of all, she had no one to help her stay calm as she edged past a dead climber just below the summit.

Norma Jean's successful solo capped more than a decade of summit attempts that began when she was a teenager. Over the years, she weathered physical setbacks, fierce storms, unprepared teammates, and the horrors of losing friends to the mountain. It was sheer grit that brought her back time and again for another attempt.

Her triumph was celebrated in the mountaineering community and memorialized in the pages of *Alaska Magazine*, the *Anchorage Daily News*, and *The Anchorage Times*. There it stopped. Her singular tale never reached the national media or unfolded in the pages of a book.

Maybe it was the qualifier next to her achievement that scared off reporters and would-be authors. After all, Norma Jean was the first solo female climber with proof that she had summited Denali.

Another woman had claimed the first-female-solo-summit title in 1982, and her name is the one on record. This, despite the fact that she produced no witnesses or photographs from the top.

Norma Jean had both.

Not long after her ascent, Norma Jean dedicated herself to other pursuits and left Alaska. Her story went dormant for over three decades. It reemerges here, in *Her Denali Solo: A Woman Alone on North America's Highest Peak*.

CHAPTER 1
# Early Ambitions

**1960s-1970s**

Mountains were not Norma Jean Marsh's first love. Music was. As a third grader at Northwood Elementary School in Anchorage in 1967, she began playing violin. She took to it easily and practiced without being prompted. Her parents enrolled her in private lessons, although it was a challenge financially. Later, she began playing in the Anchorage Youth Symphony and then the Anchorage Symphony Orchestra. Her life and her friendships revolved around music.

However, the 1970s was a dicey time to be a young person in the state. Construction of the Alaska Pipeline brought workers—mostly men—from around the country and created a rowdy, wild-west atmosphere in Alaska's cities. Violent crime doubled between the years 1970 and 1974 in Anchorage. Norman and Jean Marsh worried that their three children were not safe, especially their teenage daughter. They moved the family 40 miles northeast to the farm town of Palmer.

No longer able to play in the Anchorage Symphony and torn from her lifelong friends, Norma Jean tried to fit in; at Palmer High School, you were either a druggie or a jock. She was neither.

Cross-country skiing was part of the curriculum in P.E. class. It became a bright spot in each day as she strapped the skis onto her winter boots and glided over the athletic fields around the school. She bought a wooden pair of skis at an Army & Navy Surplus and began exploring from home. As she traveled Palmer's meadows and farmlands, she sometimes gazed off into the mountains. If only she could ski up into them. What would it be like to stand up there, looking down on the ordinary world? Freezing, for sure, but she'd bet the drama and the beauty would be worth it. Better than being stuck down here in a windy valley with people who ignored you.

In the school library one day during 10th grade, she paged through a copy of the local paper. A news clip caught her attention. A mountaineer named Bill Glude would guide a group of novices up Mt. McKinley, as Denali was known back then. He needed young people to join his team. She jumped to her feet and re-read the blurb. *Newcomers welcome!* The man would teach them everything they needed to know. Here was the opportunity she didn't know she'd been waiting for.

First, though, she would need permission. Climbing mountains was far beyond her family's realm of experience. Mother would never say yes, not in a gazillion years. Dad might.

Norman Marsh had always been his children's cheerleader.

"Yes, go for it!" and "You should definitely explore that!" he would often say. He had recently added another expression: "I wish I'd done such a thing while I still could."

Two years earlier, he had survived a workplace explosion that had left him with third-degree burns and later rheumatoid arthritis. Recovery was slow and incomplete, but his disability intensified his enthusiasm for just about everything his children wanted to try. Allowing his 16-year-old daughter to climb Denali was no exception.

"Think of how educational it will be," he said to his wife.

Jean, a school board member and PTA president, could hardly argue.

It was in the spring of 1975 that Norma Jean began training for a guided, educational expedition on North America's tallest mountain.

She bought a backpack and wore it on hikes, which she squeezed in anytime she could. Steep trails were her favorites; the sharper the grade, the better to train her lungs. She went on long bike rides. She ran. Anything to get in shape for Denali.

One day as she was biking along the Glenn Highway, she got ready to cross. Her plan was to continue onto a road that came to a T at the highway. A red car with "Coca Cola" scrawled across its doors sat at the intersection with its left blinker on. The driver looked both ways but somehow failed to spot her. As she pedaled across the Glenn, the car rammed into her.

She turned her bike in sync with the vehicle for a second, straining to stay upright and out from under the wheels. Knocked to the pavement, she suffered a gash to her head and severe road rash everywhere else. Nothing was broken, and the driver paid her medical bills and bought her a new bike, but her participation in the Bill Glude expedition was officially dead.

Over the past several months, she had managed to patch the violin-shaped hole in her life, first with a newfound love for skiing and then with dreams of mountaineering. It was going to be a long wait—one that sounded especially agonizing to a teenager—before she could attempt to climb Denali. But when she was ready, the mountain would still be there.

## CHAPTER 2
# First Expedition

**April 1980**

Norma Jean's first expedition took place not on Denali but 10 miles off its southeast flank. It was April 1980. She was age 21, three years past high school, and still hungry for time in the mountains. With her were 20-year-old climbers Dave Kempher and Grant Henke, whose friendships she had cultivated at the University of Alaska Anchorage gym over the winter, and their friend Patrick. She referred to them collectively as "the boys."

As the smallest expedition member, Norma Jean was positioned in the tail of the bush plane (a practice that's no longer done). Without enough room to fully sit up, she draped herself over the gear and craned her neck to see out the windows. The cabin fell silent as pilot Doug Geeting flew them north up the 40-mile-long Ruth Glacier. Its surface was a deceptively smooth mantle of snow in places; in others it revealed ice that was bunched and pocked with crevasses. Along the Ruth's edges were striated granite peaks. Denali loomed in the distance.

Geeting banked west around 7,650-foot Mt. Barrille, and they descended into one of the valleys in the Don Sheldon Amphitheater. Everyone stayed quiet, and Norma Jean wondered if the others also felt overwhelmed by the scale of their surroundings. She hadn't done any climbing outside of the Chugach Range, but the boys had. Dave and Grant had spent most of the spring at Yosemite, and Grant had been part of an earlier Ruth Glacier expedition.

The pilot reached overhead and cranked a lever to lower the landing gear. Two fat pontoon-like skis clicked into position below the plane's wheels.

The Cessna floated down onto a flat stretch of snow. It glided for half a minute until friction and drag brought it to a gentle stop.

Geeting's hand shot up as he instructed, "Stay put!"

He exited the plane. He opened the passenger door and reached in to grab Grant's arm. Then Dave's. Then Patrick's.

"Don't touch anything! Not even your gear."

Norma Jean had heard that bush pilots did not want their clients' help. It was all too easy to damage a plane and keep the pilot from taking off again. Geeting took Norma Jean's forearm and steered her out the door. Sunlight pricked the backs of her eyeballs, and she fished her glacier glasses out of a pocket.

Geeting tossed their gear out like a farmer baling hay: boxes and backpacks and duffel bags, skis and ropes and climbing shoes. The team picked it all up and carried it away from the landing strip. Their comings and goings scuffed up the otherwise pristine snow.

"It's just our footprints," Norma Jean observed. "Nobody else's."

"Your nearest neighbors are climbing Mt. Huntington," Geeting said. "An entire glacier system away."

He continued. "They were brushing up on their skills here first, and there's a cave they dug somewhere. Looks like it got snowed over."

"We'll watch our step," said one of the boys.

As the plane made a wide turn and moved into position for takeoff, Norma Jean could no longer hold off the jitters. This place, this *amphitheater*, was more massive than she could have imagined. And what an angry, snarling noise a bush plane made as it taxied. If it took that much power to get in and out of here, did humans really belong?

The plane accelerated down the makeshift landing strip and lifted into the air. She swallowed hard, picked up a load of gear, and took a few steps. The snow gave way.

Oh, God, a crevasse?

She fell forward, screaming into the darkness. The bottom came quickly, and it was surprisingly soft. She pushed herself up and got to her knees.

"Help!" she hollered. "HELP!"

She wiped her glacier glasses clean. The boys peered down at her. Grant elbowed Dave in the ribs. Patrick put his hands around his mouth like a megaphone.

"You found the snow cave!" he yelled.

The hole was only about three-feet deep. The boys padded off while Norma Jean floundered and fumbled her way out. Would it be so hard for someone to offer a hand?

A few minutes later, she was standing next to them, brushing the last of the snow off her pants. The boys were already busy digging out a campsite and building a snow wall around it. She rooted out a saw and shovel from her gear and joined in. It was hard not to stop and gaze at the expanse of white glacier and black rock.

To the east was a nunatak—the tip of a mountain poking out of the glacier—and on its crest was a hexagonal cabin that climbers sometimes slept in. The Mountain House was built by legendary bush pilot Don Sheldon and his friends in 1966. The boys and Norma Jean had agreed ahead of time not to use it, wanting to improve their camping skills.

She was shaping the last of the snow blocks when Grant pulled her tent—her brand new, North Face, state-of-the-art dome tent—out of the gear pile. She had just bought it from REI on her employee discount, and she couldn't help feeling a little protective. Grant and Dave began erecting it. She shook of the impulse to stop them and take over. No biggie, really, except it would have been polite to ask first, or to see if she wanted to take the lead on setting it up. Well, maybe this is how it went when you were part of a climbing team. A my-gear-is-your-gear kind of mentality.

Stationing herself at a corner, she assembled a pole and threaded it through the sleeves along the top. Dave caught the end and planted it. The four worked in concert, adding the rainfly and anchoring everything to the snow.

The group excavated a "kitchen" a few feet away from the tent area. Once the walls, benches and cooking shelf were sculpted, Norma Jean found her cookpot and heaped snow into it. She unpacked her stove system, connecting the gas cannister and priming it before lighting the stove. Then she balanced the pot on top of the support prongs and placed the foil wind barrier around the flame.

The boys sat on the snow benches they had constructed and watched her.

"Like a pro!" someone said.

She smiled and made her way to the gear pile. Many of the storage bags were the same, and it was hard to remember which ones contained the hundreds of packs of dehydrated dinners.

"Can someone add snow to the pot?" she called.

But they were deep in conversation and no one answered.

"Hey!" she called.

There was a pause. "Uh, yeah. Got it."

She carried some of the food pouches back and tossed each person two. They ripped off the tops and lined them up on a snow shelf. She returned with the pot and aimed hot water into each pouch.

The map of the Ruth Glacier area lay open on the snow. Grant folded it up and set it aside.

That night, it was hard to sleep. Light infiltrated the tent, and someone was snoring, but it was mostly the excitement that kept her up. She was on a genuine mountaineering expedition. She was lying on a glacier, for Pete's sake!

She got up several times to pee. The latrine they had dug was about 50 crevasse-free feet from the tent. Colorful wands marked the way, though she didn't need them on such a clear night. The sky only dimmed, never fully darkened, and the moon reflected off the snow.

Exhausted from a night of overstimulation, Norma Jean was the last to awaken. She tapped the empty sleeping bags beside her and sat upright.

The boys' voices, quieter than usual, were coming from the kitchen dugout. The hissing of the stove garbled their words. She dressed swiftly and slipped out of the tent.

The boys sat on the snow benches and encircled the map. They looked up. Faces reddened.

"Look who's up!" Dave said.

"Good morning," said Grant. "Nice bedhead."

She patted her hair down, feeling strands stick to her mittens. Why hadn't anyone gotten her up? She pursed her lips.

"Where're we headed to first?"

The boys exchanged looks. A breeze wisped through the dugout, and the map crinkled in response. Grant shook it out and resettled it. He met her gaze.

"Well, it's not really a matter of 'we,'" he said, drawing a line in the air between the group and her. He then pantomimed a circle that included just himself and the other boys. "It's a matter of 'we.'—the existing climbing trio."

She tilted her head.

"Just you guys?"

"Yes," Grant said while the others' heads bobbed in agreement.

This was the first she'd heard of this new definition of "we."

"We've all studied the map," Dave said. "For hours and hours. But you haven't."

That wasn't true; she had pored over hers at home every chance she got. She opened her mouth to protest.

"And all of us," Patrick said, "have more climbing experience than you."

"And how am I supposed to get that experience?" she snapped.

"Just let us check out some routes," Dave said. "Make sure it's safe enough first. Then you can come."

The whoosh of a distant avalanche echoed through the amphitheater, as if timed to underscore Dave's point.

"A team is only as strong as its weakest link," said Patrick.

Norma Jean felt the steam rise in her head. She crossed her arms and looked to the side. The boys sure did like using her tent and stove, but they couldn't be bothered to let her climb with them?

She was getting played.

• • •

She was a realist, though. Trying to force her way onto the boys' team wasn't going to work. She would bide her time in camp and prod them in the evenings until they relented.

Each day, she occupied herself with her map, identifying the features around the landing strip and plotting routes up the peaks. She studied the sky and observed the shapes and movements of the clouds. She calibrated her findings with the weather that followed.

A whump. A pause. Then a soft rumble like distant thunder. The noises signaled an avalanche, and several times a day, she stopped whatever she was doing to scan the mountains. Sometimes she could see the telltale powder cloud rising into the sky.

She kept snow off the tent and made hot drinks in the evenings. The boys toyed with inviting her along on a couple of ski tours but never up any mountains. She spent most of her waking hours in camp alone. By the end of the first week, her anger had resurfaced.

Then something unexpected happened.

The boys were scrutinizing the map, dissecting various approaches to various slopes, while Norma Jean hung close and tried to predict which excuse they would make for leaving her behind. Would it be the tired refrain of "This looks like an expert route" or the newest addition, "You're not strong enough"?

The only human sounds they had heard over the past seven days had been their own. So it came as a shock to hear a voice, tinny and far away. Norma Jean and the boys froze. A few seconds passed before they heard it again.

"Hello," or maybe "Hey-oh."

All sat upright. They jumped to their feet, bodies moving as one, and snaked out of the dugout. Their camp sat at the bottom of Pittock Pass, and the voice was coming from somewhere much higher up. Sunlight blazed over the ridge. Norma Jean cupped her hands around her sunglasses and squinted up with watering eyes. Three dots were descending the pass, and in no time, their shapes became decipherable. The men wound their way down, moving deliberately around crevasses, with little to no hesitation.

Experts.

She gaped, as did the boys. One of the strangers waved, setting off a unanimous, double-armed response in her group. Then they bolted out of camp and clambered toward the strangers. It was challenging for her to keep up. The snow was deep and every fourth or fifth step was a post-hole. The boys reached the skiers first. She arrived after the introductions.

"And who's this?" asked a handsome guy with a moustache.

She introduced herself.

"I'm Geoff," said the skier. "And this is Josh and Bill. We're from the Harvard Mountaineering Club."

"Ohhhh!" she said, impressed by the credential. "So nice to meet you. And such a surprise. If we'd have known you were coming, we would have vacuumed."

The Harvard men laughed.

"We climbed a new route on Mt. Huntington," Geoff said. "Decided to come back this way for better ski terrain."

Norma Jean swallowed. Geoff sounded sort of casual about it, but "coming back this way" meant climbing over several miles of intimidating terrain.

One of the boys motioned to the Harvard men to follow. Back in camp, the newcomers dug out a spot nearby and put up their tent. They joined Norma Jean and the boys in the kitchen dugout and accepted their offers of dinner.

Geoff, Josh, and Bill were in their mid-twenties, but they radiated maturity. The reason was hard to pin down. Possibly it was the lack of bravado and one-upmanship. Maybe it was the way they pitched in with all types of chores, adding snow to the cookpot, collecting the group's trash, chinking the snow walls, before anyone else thought of it.

The conversation turned to mountains around the Ruth that neither group had climbed. The boys detailed some of their grand schemes. The men responded thoughtfully when they had information to share.

Norma Jean took advantage of a short pause.

"So, what's your plan?" she asked the Harvard guys. "Which one's next?"

"Looks like Mt. Dan Beard," Geoff answered.

All eyes turned toward the blocky granite dome across the glacier, a uniquely weird mountain flanked by two armlike ridges that looked like they were reaching out to you. Geoff tapped the map. He traced his finger over the terrain lines. Then he pulled back and looked at Norma Jean.

"What's a good route," he asked, "in your opinion?"

She cocked her head and looked him in the face. *Me?*

He waited.

Well, this was a first. Her face grew hot. But she had been studying this map for days and had spent hours creating an aspirational climb of Mt. Dan Beard.

She leaned in and pointed to the mountain's southwest arm. "Start here," she said. "Then up to the ridgeline, turn at the top, and follow it on up from there." The route seemed logical from the little she knew about the terrain.

Harvard nodded in unison.

"We're leaving at 5 a.m.," Josh said. "Come with us, Norma Jean."

She smiled with her whole face.

"I'd love to."

• • •

The next morning, she woke at 3:30. The twilight revealed a mass of sleeping bodies in mummy bags. The boys had declared they weren't coming to Mt. Dan Beard.

"Rest day," they had said.

She rolled her eyes. "Cooties," she thought. It was screamingly obvious they just didn't want to climb with her.

A soft rustling came from the Harvard tent.

Norma Jean turned on her headlamp and re-checked the gear she had assembled last night before bed. She slipped out of the tent. Her small cookpot was preloaded with just enough snow for a single serving of oatmeal.

After breakfast, she crammed her sleeping bag back into its stuff-sack and added it to her pack. She resisted the urge to check her gear a third time. Instead, she ferried the whole lot to a spot outside the camp walls. She plunked down her backpack and attended to her skis.

Reaching Mt. Dan Beard meant traversing nearly three miles across the Ruth Glacier. In addition to crevasses, the glacier was full of sloping terrain. Traveling on it required attaching an accessory called "skins" to the undersides of her skis. Made of mohair, the skins allowed her to ski uphill without slipping backward.

She hoisted her pack and clicked into her bindings just as Geoff, Josh, and Bill skied up. They exchanged good-mornings, and Norma Jean's adrenaline-soaked voice drowned out theirs. She hadn't meant to holler.

"I'm a little nervous," she admitted.

The men murmured assurances, and someone patted her on the back.

Geoff ran down a gear list, and she verified that she had each item. She had not forgotten a single thing.

"Your skins are on?" he asked.

She tilted a ski so he could see the underside. "Yes," she said. "Though this will be my first time using them on a glacier."

"You wore them in the Chugach, right?"

"Yes."

She resisted saying more, afraid the words would tumble out and she would be "that girl who talked too much," as she often felt around the boys. Yet she did worry about whether she had enough experience for this excursion.

"It won't feel that different. Just keep your feet flat when going upslope."

Geoff certainly had confidence in her. All of them were treating her like an experienced mountaineer who knew what the hell she was doing.

They tied together in teams of two, each pair connected by 50 feet of rope. As they worked, the cold penetrated Norma Jean's jacket and wind pants. She was dressed in light layers for skiing, not standing.

"Let's go," Geoff said.

Josh followed. Norma Jean went next and her rope partner Bill picked up the rear.

She moved self-consciously. Skiing on skins and wearing a heavy pack stunted her strides. She watched Josh's legs and copied him. Then she found her own rhythm, slightly faster for her shorter legs. But the sight of an open crevasse—a black, human-sized gash in the snow—transformed her worries. Was her backpack too big? Did it make her top-heavy? What if she lost her balance?

The path sloped upward, and she changed to shorter, faster strides. Instead of carrying her to safety, her skis started backsliding. She side-eyed the crevasse and dug in her poles. She would grind her way up this hill. She would not let this glacier swallow her.

"Norma Jean," Bill called from behind. "Get off your edges."

"What?" she yelled back. "Oh!"

She flattened her skis, and the skins caught. Thank heavens. She skied up the hill, distancing herself from the abyss. Now she just had to remember to keep doing it the right way.

• • •

The guys weren't kidding when they said it might feel like a long trek to her. Each hour lent weight to her pack. Her confidence sagged.

Would her legs recover in time for tomorrow's climb? Did she have the chops to make it all the way to the summit? She had spent a couple of summers guiding novice climbers up peaks in the Chugach Range outside of Anchorage and Palmer, but she'd never done anything like this.

The sun rose high overhead, and the group stopped to shed layers. From here in the middle of the glacier, they could no longer see their route. Geoff and Josh consulted the map, then showed Norma Jean where they were. It took deliberate concentration for her to absorb the information.

She fell back into line, quad muscles screaming, and followed Josh across a series of rises. Most of the crevasses were camouflaged by snow, but now and again they passed another open hole. Her heart revved each time, and each time she recentered her eyes on Josh's back.

Mt. Dan Beard's granite torso was farther away than it looked. Getting there required endless crisscrossing. There was no such thing as "as the crow flies" when skiing on a glacier. Ten hours after they had set out, they ascended the pocket glacier partly encircled by the mountain. They stood still, breathing hard as they scoured the area. Norma Jean knew they had to choose their camp with care. Crevasses were an obvious concern, and jumbles of rocks and ice were piled up around the base of the mountain, evidence of its frequent avalanches.

They found a spot that reminded her a little of their camp by Pittock Pass, but this place was different, not just in location, but in personal significance. This camp would be the one from which Norma Jean would, at long last, make her first climb off the Ruth Glacier.

## CHAPTER 3
# Mt. Dan Beard

Norma Jean lay motionless in the early hours. A sound sleep had recharged her body after yesterday's never-ending glacier crossing. Anticipation of the climb ahead was pulling her out of a dreamy haze. Geoff and Bill stirred, while Josh, too, lay still in the twilight.

As the tent grew brighter, she sat up. She got out of her sleeping bag and slipped into her heavy coat, then unzipped the rainfly. She padded along the snow in her down booties, following the team's wands to the latrine area they had marked off last night. She returned minutes later to a bustle of activity. Each man had taken on a different task. Geoff was priming the stove; Josh was rolling up sleeping bags inside the tent; and Bill was examining their climbing gear.

"After breakfast, we're packing up camp," Geoff told her. "We will carry it all up there with us."

She nodded. Spending a night on the mountain was probably unavoidable, especially with a newbie on the team. Without her, the three men might have powered up and down in a day.

She crawled back into the tent and took out her climbing clothes. It was important not to sweat today, so she chose her lightweight, polypropylene long johns and shirt. A pair of GORE-TEX pants would serve as a shell from the elements. Gaiters would keep the snow out of her boots and protect her pants from getting caught in the teethlike crampons she would strap to her soles. On top, she would wear a tan fleece jacket under her GORE-TEX coat.

She unpacked her gloves, over-mitts, socks, and boot liners. When she extracted a pair of clean undies and jog bra, Josh raised his eyebrows and crawled out of the tent. The team dismantled their camp and distributed the gear among the backpacks. They secured their skis and marked them with a wand in case it snowed. On the short trek to Dan Beard's southwest arm, Norma Jean pressed her crampons into the hard-packed snow. They bit in reassuringly.

Her legs were spring-loaded, and her mind was sharp. This was really going to happen. A team of climbers—Harvard climbers—was preparing to follow a route that she had mapped out just 36 hours ago.

They roped up. Geoff went first, and he pierced the snow with his probe to check for crevasses every few steps. As the glacier sloped upward, he stepped to the side and held out the lead rack—a tightly woven nylon sling with carefully selected climbing tools dangling from carabiners. The metal nuts, hexes, and snow screws clinked together like wrist bangles.

She clipped the rack to her harness and hoped Geoff didn't notice the quivering in her hands. His face betrayed nothing as he took two snow pickets, slid them into a side pocket on her pack, and strapped them in. Straight ahead, a rock face contained a long diagonal crack. Norma Jean selected a wedge-shaped nut and worked it into the narrow space. She clipped it to her rope and then did a double take. Something else, brown with rust, was sticking out of the crack: a loop that was partly eroded away.

"Hey!" she said, turning to Geoff. "Is that an old piton?"

He ran a gloved finger over it. "So, it is."

The team gathered round.

"I guess we're not the first to attempt ole Dan Beard," Bill said.

Norma Jean smiled. Bill's observation brought a measure of relief and validation: She had chosen the same route as some earlier, more seasoned climbers.

Geoff helped her set the nut, and he belayed her as she climbed the sloped wall to a snowy section. Some 40 feet above, a line divided the snow into upper and lower sections. It took a moment to realize this was the bergschrund, a crevasse that formed between the moving ice of the glacier and the stationary ice of the mountain. Crossing it would be a new experience, and a nerve-racking one if she thought too hard about it.

The team approached, keeping a respectful distance from the meandering gash in the snow that narrowed here and widened there.

Geoff would go first, and he took back the lead rack. The team moved downslope, and Bill volunteered to serve as the anchor. If the snow around the bergschrund collapsed, Bill would counterbalance Geoff's weight. Gravity would work in their favor.

Norma Jean observed, unblinking and shallow-breathed, as Geoff approached the crevasse. A few quick strides took him safely across. He climbed higher and waved down at them.

She exhaled. "Whew!"

Bill nodded knowingly as he reeled in the rope. He turned to Josh. "You're next."

Josh's crossing felt slightly less perilous to Norma Jean, but still, she didn't relax until he clambered up beside Geoff.

Was she next? If so, how would Bill get across?

"They're going to belay us from up above," he said. "First you, then me."

Higher up, Geoff and Josh began digging out an anchor system. They attached the rope to a picket and buried it. Bill released the rope from his harness and handed it to Norma Jean, watching as she attached it to hers. He checked her knot and snugged it. Geoff waved again and Norma Jean made her way up. The rope stayed taut, but Geoff was careful not to drag her.

She stood at the gap and counted to three. Only a couple of feet wide, the crevasse didn't look as terrifying as she had imagined. Wind and gravity had created a white blanket that hid its depths. She reached the wall of snow on the other side and scaled it. In moments, she joined Geoff and Josh, and soon Bill followed. They roped together in pairs: Norma Jean with Josh and Geoff with Bill.

"You lead off," Geoff said, handing back the rack.

Norma Jean led three pitches up the southwest flank of Mt. Dan Beard. Although each one lent her a little more confidence, she eyed the icy overhanging rock above them with dread. They were in a couloir, with no obvious way around this monolith. What to do now?

As she waited for Josh to reach her, she turned and took in the view. The Ruth Glacier spanned out below, and on the other side was the camp they had left yesterday morning. She could even make out her yellow and tan dome tent and the kitchen dugout. The boys were probably still asleep.

Josh rose closer. She envied his confident steps and ease with the ice axe.

"What's going on?" he called up to her. "Why did you stop?"

Her face grew hot. She looked up again at the outcropping and studied its features for a clue. If only she didn't have to say the words. If only he would just take the lead and not make it a big deal.

She grimaced. "I don't know how to climb over that."

Josh tilted his head and pursed his lips. Luckily, his eyes weren't visible through his glacier glasses. Norma Jean imagined him squinting with scorn.

His voice, however, was soft and forgiving. "Okay, just give me the lead rack. I'll take us up."

She unhooked the rack and gingerly handed it off. Josh took a couple of steps up. He worked his left hand into a fissure in the rock and sank his axe into a span of ice on the right. He muscled his way up and over the rock in a way that made it look easy. Norma Jean let him get higher before copying his moves.

The team took turns leading. Norma Jean observed the others' techniques and learned on the go. Maybe someday it would all come naturally.

As they regrouped, she overheard Geoff and Bill talking about the likelihood of avalanches.

"I don't like the slope angle," Geoff said.

Bill nodded. "Me, either. I'm afraid it's going to let go."

They leaned into the mountain, contemplating.

"It's no safer to go back down," Geoff said. "Everything is warming up."

He began climbing higher.

Norma Jean felt removed from the danger, somehow, as though their worries didn't affect her. Her stomach grumbled and her feet ached and her brain was tired from making a thousand decisions. Though the men were polite about it, her lack of experience was getting more obvious with each pitch. She tried to shake off the malaise and focus on the positives. Look around, she instructed herself. Appreciate the view. Is there anything more beautiful than sunshine on snow?

She felt the avalanche before she saw it. The ground rumbled. She whipped her head back. Geoff was in the lead, about 60 feet above her on the rope. He faced down toward her, eyes and mouth wide. He stood on his own island while the slope broke on either side of him.

The slide knocked her off her feet, slamming her face down and carrying her a couple of yards. Snow plugged her mouth, nose, and ears before it solidified. Her heart pounded in her temples. It was dark and she couldn't move.

She was not buried deep. Her backpack stuck out, and the rope connecting her to the others had not broken. Miraculously, Josh and Bill had managed to keep themselves from going under by using a swimming technique, and Geoff had stayed on his feet. The three rushed to her and shoveled the snow from her face. They scratched and scraped and pried and yanked until she lifted her head and gasped.

The slope around them had been scoured, but both below and above, the avalanche danger remained. If the team could reach the rocky ridge just 500 feet up, they could make camp and start again in the safety of the early morning cold.

Geoff pointed to the part of the slope that was still covered in snow. He voiced what everyone knew.

"The trouble is," he said, "we have to cross *that* in order to get up there. I think when we set foot on it, it's going to go."

Josh nodded. "Yeah. But what choice do we have? Everything we climbed earlier is soft now. Going down could be even worse."

Norma Jean, blinking away the flashbacks and trembling, tried to focus on the present. Were they stuck on this naked rock, vulnerable to the next avalanche?

The men rechecked the ropes and ensured the knots were secure. The team stepped lightly onto the snow, with Geoff in the lead and Bill in the rear, but the weight of four people was too much. The snowy expanse fractured. It broke away, knocking them to their knees. Norma Jean scrambled upward as the slide pulled her closer to the cliff. She regained her footing and leaned into the rock for stability. Head down, she had a narrow view between her feet of the snow disappearing over the edge.

"Holy hell!" yelled one of the men.

"Oh, my God," said another.

Everyone grew quiet, though Norma Jean was hyperventilating. Spots dappled her vision.

"It's okay," Geoff said. "We're safe now."

The rest of the slope had been swept clean. Only rock and ice remained.

• • •

Hours later, they made it to the top of the southwest arm. Setting up camp on the narrow, corniced ridge required time and creativity. There was no room for a tent, so Geoff and Josh dug a cave in the snow. The floor was barely wide enough for four bodies. They took turns laying out their foam pads and sleeping bags in the dark little cavity. Then they spent the evening crouched together outside on the ridge. Surviving two avalanches had stirred up a need for human contact, and nestling together provided the tiniest bit of reassurance.

Clouds floated in below, and the setting sun tinted them pink.

"Hate to wreck the mood," Bill said, "but I hope we aren't in for a storm tonight."

They all nodded in response. What was there to say? They had bested Mother Nature today—twice. She might just whip up some retaliatory wind and snow.

When the sun dipped out of sight, the climbers filed into the shelter on hands and knees. They stayed roped together. That way, no one getting up to pee in the middle of the night risked falling to their death. The only light came from the tiny entrance.

Despite the discomfort of lying fully harnessed among coils of rope, Norma Jean slept hard.

Someone's snoring woke her. For the first time since arriving at the Ruth, she found herself in complete darkness. Weird. She turned on her headlamp and saw the dusting of white on their sleeping bags—and much, much worse, the snow piled up inside the doorway. Bill must have been right about the storm.

"You guys!" Norma Jean said.

The others woke. Geoff propped himself up on his elbows and looked around.

"The door is covered," she said. "Are we buried?"

Geoff crawled toward the entrance and began clawing at it. He broke through just as Bill reached up and punched a hole in the ceiling. Fresh air rushed in.

"Let's get out of here!" Geoff said.

One at a time, they dragged themselves out into the bright, early-morning light. A west wind stung their faces, but there was no storm. The snow clogging their doorway was just spindrift that had blown in while they slept. Even now, white swirls spun off the mountains surrounding them. The bulbous ice on Dan Beard's summit dome glistened, and below, clouds receded like an ebbing tide. Conditions were perfect, and no one even had to ask if they would continue on to the summit. They could worry about the descent later, at some distant point in the day.

They planned their way to the top. The route would take them through more mixed climbing of snow, ice, and rock. Summiting from here had to be done in one, long push. There were no other places to stop.

Intense concentration and physical effort made the hours flow. One moment they were rock climbing, and Geoff was giving her pointers on working nuts and hexes into the cracks, and the next they were plodding through hip-deep sugar snow. She learned how to place pickets (which looked like long arrows) and flukes (which looked like shovel blades) in the snow to help anchor the team against falls.

Nearer to the top, the snow hardened into ice. The dome reminded her of the cap of a giant mushroom. It was her turn to lead, but the terrain was far above her ability level. She asked Geoff to take her place as they pushed to the summit.

"Of course," he said. "I'd be grateful."

After a short rest, he started up the bulge. The rope unspooled slowly at first. Then, in an indication that the angle had softened, it moved swiftly upward. In no time, Geoff's triumphant "YEEEEE HAWWWWW!" announced he had arrived.

The team whooped in response.

"Your turn, Norma Jean."

Her first summit on this Ruth Glacier expedition. Such a pivotal moment. A tingling sensation started in her scalp and spread all the way to her fingertips and toes.

"I can't believe it."

She checked her knots and ropes and took a big step upward. Swinging her ice axe forced her to lean backward, and her heavy pack toyed with her balance. Though the guys had her on a tight rope, it felt like she might just fall into the 3,000 feet of nothingness between her and the Ruth Glacier.

But her axe blade sank into the ice and she followed up with two small steps. The next sequence was harder. She paused, then climbed a foot higher. Then a little more. Another pause to gather her wits.

The rope went tight, and suddenly she was being pulled onto her belly and up over the worst of the hump. She found her footing again, relieved to see that the long slope ahead wasn't nearly as steep. Stomping her crampons into the ice, she followed Geoff to the summit. Soon the others trudged up from behind. Everyone high-fived and hugged.

They sat down to rest and identify the peaks lining the Don Sheldon Amphitheater.

Josh fished a can of condensed milk out of his pack. He pierced a drinking hole and an air hole in the top and handed it to Norma Jean.

"The best thing you'll ever taste," he said.

She raised her eyebrows. In her house, the white and red tins had been one of those things that remained in the pantry between trips to the grocery store. Her mother used it to make fudge or pudding or something.

She took a sip, then a gulp. It was liquid candy.

"Oh, Lordy," she said, throwing her head back for effect. "Sweet heaven in my mouth!"

They laughed. She passed the can to Geoff.

"Look," said Bill. He pointed toward the amphitheater. "Your base camp."

Norma Jean wiped milk off her upper lip. She wondered if the boys were venturing up another mountain today.

Geoff followed her gaze. He smirked and shook his head slowly.

"I cannot wait to tell those guys you summited," he said. "It's going to blow their minds."

• • •

A distant storm front motivated the team to cut their celebration short. What the descent lacked in physical strain, it made up for in terror. The down climb over the mushroom cap brought out curses and even a few quiet whimpers. The team retraced their steps, staying on a short rope over the rocky parts and moving as a single unit over less steep terrain. At the site of yesterday's avalanches, Bill belayed them one-by-one over the crown face. They moved swiftly along the 30-degree slope to a rock buttress, where they set up new anchors. By late afternoon, they were descending the long couloir that led to the glacier, and at sunset, they gained their original tent site in the high glacier cirque.

Norma Jean was stoked. Adrenaline and a few handfuls of GORP powered her back across the glacier in just a few hours. They skied into camp in the Sheldon Amphitheater after midnight. The others awoke and emerged from the tent to greet them.

Geoff was right: The boys' facial expressions were a study in disbelief. Dave's brows were arched high over wide eyes. Patrick's glove covered his mouth. Grant cocked his head.

"You summited?" he asked.

She nodded. "We did!"

An awkward pause followed, and Norma Jean felt compelled to fill it.

"It's not like it was easy," she said. "We got caught in two avalanches."

The boys continued to stare. Had they even heard her?

"Two of them," she said. "Without dying."

Someone coughed.

Exhaustion caught up to Norma Jean. The physical and mental strain of the past 48 hours had been brutal, and it was topped off by skiing and skinning across the glacier with barely a break. The boys' disbelief annoyed her. It wasn't her job to convince them that she had summited. To hell with them.

"I need sleep," she said, turning to the men. "Let's get the tent up."

When she woke at eight the next morning, her climbing partners were sprawled out around her. The only noise came from outside the tent.

It was clear from the conversation that the boys had been talking about the Dan Beard climb. They had moved past their disbelief about Norma Jean's summit. Now they were in "if she can do it, we can do it" territory.

"We gotta get more details," Grant said.

"Agreed," said Dave. "Maybe they'll wake up soon."

With that, she closed her eyes and went back to sleep.

## CHAPTER 4
# A Tragic End

Norma Jean wedged the last of her camping equipment into her backpack and listened to the discussion about Mt. Dan Beard. The Harvard men had tried to deter Grant and Dave, but the boys seemed deaf to all the warnings about avalanches. They were young, strong, and quick, and they had just enough time to squeeze in a final ascent. Might as well make it a challenging one. They would climb early, before the slopes heated up and released their loads.

Norma Jean buckled her pack and went to stand with the group as they studied the map. Patrick, who would stay back at the Mountain House on the ridge, kept himself slightly apart.

Geoff lay the map across a tarp, and they all bent over for a closer look. He pointed to the site of their snow cave.

"Dig in here for the night," he said. "Then travel light to the top. Don't linger."

Grant and Dave nodded. Their skis lay ready to step into, poles standing up beside them.

"Safe travels, you two," Norma Jean said. "Do you have enough food?"

Grant gave her a sharp hug that forced the air from her lungs. He stepped back. "Four days' worth, like you suggested."

She cracked a smile.

Dave hugged her an instant longer. "Thanks for letting us borrow your tent. We'll take good care of it."

"You're welcome. And I know you will."

The sound of a Cessna engine whined in the distance. She inspected her gear pile; everything was accounted for.

An hour later, she and the Harvard men were in the air. The small plane's rapid ascent made her stomach tingle and drew her deeper into her seat. Contentment rippled through her. Below, she glimpsed the boys skiing across the glacier—two thimble-sized figures under bulging backpacks. The expedition had not turned out the way she had expected. After all, who could have imagined the Harvard team materializing at the top of Pittock Pass, inviting her to join them on Dan Beard, and then flying out together? But it was all right. Everyone had gotten what they needed.

She and the men rented bunks in the Fairview Inn in Talkeetna, which served as a way station for Denali climbers. They aired out their tent, clothes, and sleeping bags. They examined their ropes for frays and checked the integrity of their hardware.

The camaraderie was the best part, of course, but the beer and generous portions of food enhanced the post-climb experience. Norma Jean was a real climber now—and only now did she feel confident telling Geoff, Josh, and Bill about her next move.

"In about three weeks," she confessed, "I'm joining an all-women's group on Denali. I wasn't sure I was capable, but thanks to you guys, I think I am."

Geoff's mouth fell open for an instant before morphing into a smile. "That's awesome," he said. "Stellar!"

"You are going to learn so much," Josh said.

Bill leaned over and clinked his mug with hers.

• • •

It was a Monday night, some days after she had returned to her parents' house in Palmer. The phone rang, and her mother picked up.

"No. This is Jean," she responded. "I'll get her."

Norma Jean hurried down the stairs.

"Who is it?" she whispered.

"Geoff," her mother mouthed back.

Her face opened into a smile as she took the receiver.

"Hey, Geoff!"

On the other end, he cleared his throat and went quiet.

"Geoff?"

"It's about Grant and Dave," he said, voice cracking. "They're missing."

She grabbed the banister for support. Her legs—at peak strength from skiing and climbing—would no longer support her. She eased herself to the floor.

"Missing from Dan Beard?"

A few seconds passed. "Yes."

"Since when?"

"Friday."

She pressed her fingers to her lips. Tears fell in the shared silence. Sometime later, Geoff managed to tell her that he, Josh, and Bill planned to join one of the search parties.

"I'm coming, too," she said.

She had already begun preparing for the Women on Denali Expedition, and her gear was organized. She repacked with speed and efficiency. Within eight hours, she had returned to Talkeetna. Weather kept them grounded at first, but soon she and the Harvard men were up in the air, along with a young park service ranger named Roger Robinson. He had tried to dissuade Norma Jean from being part of the search party.

They landed in the Don Sheldon Amphitheater, where they had taken off days ago, and the ranger tried once again.

"I'm begging you, please don't be part of this," he said. "It probably won't end well, and the experience will stay with you the rest of your life."

Tearing up, she glanced at him and shook her head. How could she stand by and not help? Without Grant and Dave, she might never have even come to the Ruth Glacier. She owed it to them. They had argued and goofed around, shared a tent, and eaten every meal together for weeks. The part that really gnawed at her: if it hadn't been for Norma Jean and her lucky summit, they might never have attempted Mt. Dan Beard.

The plane turned around as the team hoisted their packs, attached skins to skis, and snapped boots into bindings. She felt more confident about crossing the glacier this time. The crevasses still yawned at her, though she no longer imagined herself backsliding or toppling into them. Her purpose was clear: Get across the glacier and assist in any way she could.

They reached the cirque at the base of Dan Beard. One of the other search parties had made camp at the site of Norma Jean and the men's former basecamp. Beyond the searchers' blue tent, partially buried in snow, stood her yellow and brown dome tent that the boys had borrowed. The sight of it made her stomach lurch. She took off her skis and walked around it. She batted the snow off, allowing the tent to pop back upright, and then opened it up for a look. Empty. Not even a whiff remained of the "mountaineers' musk" they had all joked about.

Keeping their eyes on Norma Jean, the Harvard men set their gear down. Geoff removed her backpack and leaned it against the others.

"Are you all right?"

She nodded.

Roger got on the radio and set up a rendezvous point on the mountain with fellow rangers. Abruptly, he turned his back on Norma Jean and the others and walked away. The radio squawked loudly, but she couldn't make out the words. Roger stopped talking and continued facing away. Minutes passed before he came back to share what he had learned. A helicopter crew had spotted a rope near the summit, and pieces of gear had been found strewn down the mountainside.

The distant thwap of rotors made Norma Jean cringe. It was all too real. What little hope she had held for Grant and Dave sifted away.

She crawled into her empty tent and lay down, overwhelmed by memories. When Geoff joined her, she sat up, sniffled, and wiped away the tears. He knelt down and took her hand.

"We're going to go find the boys. It's a body recovery mission now."

She pulled her hand away and rolled onto her knees to get up. "I'm aware of that."

He touched her shoulder.

"I know you're strong, and I know you're determined to help. But the best action you can take in this moment is no action."

She stared at him.

"I need you to stay here," he said firmly.

She opened her mouth to argue but thought better of it. In truth, she would be a strain on their search party. Roger's warning had also sunk in. Her imagination was already summoning up gruesome images, and reality would be so much worse. Better to let Grant and Dave live on in her mind as gutsy, beautiful, young men.

Roger rolled up the searchers' blue tent and fit it into his backpack. The Harvard men stowed some of their gear with Norma Jean to lighten their loads. Speed was important in a place with capricious weather. The men roped back up and hiked toward the slope in their boots and crampons.

She knew the plan. They would climb to the saddle two to three thousand feet below the summit—the most probable resting place of the boys. Then they would have to excavate the bodies, strap them into sleds, and lower them the rest of the way down the mountain.

Without a radio, she could only guess at their progress. The high clouds descended, covering the basecamp in fog. She unwrapped some jerky and took tiny bites to calm her nerves. Hours passed. Occasionally she thought she heard men shouting, their voices disembodied and their words undecipherable. Had the boys been found?

The wind whipped up and drove her into the tent. When she finally emerged in the early morning twilight, the air was gray and soupy. She made tea and zipped herself back in.

She heard them minutes before they reached camp. No one spoke, but the crunch of footsteps and the rasp of two heavy sleds sent forth a sound she would never forget. Leaning on a ski pole for support, she stood waiting. The men's faces were twisted into various shades of misery. Their eyes didn't register her presence.

(Later she would learn the theory about what had taken Grant and Dave's lives. The two had been resting together on a cornice of snow on a high ridge. When the cornice collapsed, they fell two to three thousand feet.)

Mercifully, the bodies were wrapped and hidden from her view. One was in the blue tent that Roger had taken with him. The realization made her feel queasy. Her stomach ached, and saliva pooled in her mouth, but somehow she held it back.

"We have to get them out a little ways," Roger said. "Where the pilot can reach them."

They packed up camp wordlessly and put their skis back on. The cold, murky air pressed in, and the men's teeth chattered audibly. Whether their shivers came from sadness or the chill, she couldn't be sure.

The weather felt appropriate somehow—nature's recognition of tragedy. But, as they struggled to maneuver the sleds off the cirque at the base of Dan Beard, the sun rose over the Alaska Range and sliced through the gloom. Gaudy yellow light edged with pink and lavender shot across the glacier and spotlighted them. Eyes watering, they turned their heads from the glare.

The angle widened, and the whole scene lit up. The rays penetrated their clothes, and for the first time in hours they felt warm. Still, as they towed the bodies of Grant and Dave farther out onto the glacier, they shivered.

CHAPTER 5

# A Failure of Group Dynamics

**May 1980**

The Women on Denali Expedition was to begin just two weeks after Grant and Dave's deaths, and Norma Jean prepared for it with an intensity that chased away thoughts of anything else. At home in Palmer, she cataloged her equipment and made frequent trips to Anchorage to replace damaged or missing pieces.

Her new teammates included three guides from Colorado and one fellow Alaskan, a physical therapist named Susan. Norma Jean, as the youngest and least experienced alpinist, felt honored to be included in the group. She was climbing with professionals.

So it came as a shock when she arrived in Talkeetna the day before the team's flight to find Susan alone.

"I've been told our team already flew out," Susan said. "They're waiting for us at Kahiltna Base Camp."

Alarm bells clanged in Norma Jean's head.

"What?!"

Susan shrugged.

"Why?! Did we get the date wrong? Are we late?"

"No. The pilot said they just decided to leave early."

Norma Jean frowned. "That's weird."

Susan nodded and then took a deep breath.

"Oh, and something else. There's a man with them."

• • •

Norma Jean and Susan spent the day consolidating gear and getting to know each other. Susan had a calm and respectful manner that Norma Jean found endearing. They made a tacit agreement not to gossip about their "Women (and Random Man) on Denali" teammates or even to speculate on why they had taken off early. They must have had a good reason, and surely they would explain it all once the two caught up with them.

Another surprise awaited them later that evening. When they landed at the 7,200-foot base camp and unloaded their gear, they looked around for the Coloradoans. The camp manager informed them that the Women on Denali Expedition—with Jim in the lead—had moved on to Camp 1, about five and a half miles out the Kahiltna Glacier.

"Are you kidding me?!" Norma Jean spat. "That is rude."

Poised as ever, Susan grimaced.

"We've had a long day," she said. "Let's make camp here. We can start fresh in the morning."

The steam building in Norma Jean's head could have propelled her all the way to Camp 1 and beyond. Who did these people think they were? And who was this Jim? Why did he seem to be the one making the decisions?

Susan continued to watch her. "Take a breath," she said gently. "Cleanse your mind. Then open your eyes and take in the beauty."

Norma Jean heeded the advice.

The evening was charmed. Snow crosshatched the crags of nearby Mt. Hunter and piled up in its couloirs. Foraker loomed across the glacier, its top shrouded in white. Denali, looking less formidable in the distance, peeked through the saddle of Mt. Francis and Peak 12,200. Evening sun warming their faces, the pair traded stories about their jobs and their climbing experience. Norma Jean explained that she had lost some friends just weeks earlier but wasn't ready to talk about it.

She slept well that night; it appeared Susan hadn't moved, either. They were awakened by a very convincing mooing sound.

Cows?

Susan sat up and opened the tent fly. Side by side, they peered out to see the source of the noise. A line of tanned, hairy-faced men skied by. Their colorful gear pegged them as Europeans.

"I guess they're teasing us," Susan said with a shrug.

"Maybe they're not used to women climbers," Norma Jean suggested.

She set up the stove and went to collect snow. Choosing an untouched patch well away from the tent sites and latrines was vital.

The cookpot started to boil, and through the vapor they could see two female figures skiing toward them. They moved synchronously, with rapid pole-plants, heads bowed. They were in a rush.

They paused at a campsite to ask a question. A climber pointed in Norma Jean and Susan's direction, and the skiers headed straight toward them. Norma Jean turned off the stove and stepped out of the tent site.

The skiers were identical twins named Carol and Kathy, and they were part of the Women on Denali Expedition. They hugged Norma Jean and Susan and apologized profusely for leaving them behind.

"I'm sure it caused some confusion," Carol said.

"Not our intent," Kathy added. "We're just trying to go with the flow."

"You're going to love Erica," Carol said of the expedition's leader.

Norma Jean waited a few seconds to allow the question hovering over them to land.

"And Jim?" she asked.

Carol and Kathy locked eyes.

Finally, Carol said, "We don't know what to make of him. He and Erica hit it off in Anchorage, and he invited himself along."

"We're hoping he'll peel off and go his own way," Kathy said.

Norma Jean smirked. "Huh."

She invited the sisters to share breakfast. They agreed before she'd even finished speaking. Using borrowed bowls and spoons, they ate fast and cleaned up thoroughly. The foursome packed up the campsite and roped in together.

They began the long ski on the Kahiltna toward Camp 1 at 7,800 feet. The route started down Heartbreak Hill and made a wide bend around Mt. Frances. Norma Jean felt well-rested and happy, grateful to be united with two new teammates. Ever-present crevasses surrounded them, and hanging glaciers made it partway down nearby couloirs. Seracs marked the edges of other glaciers like ice turrets guarding a castle. The world sparkled blue and white, and only the whoosh of skis on snow broke the silence.

To her relief, Norma Jean easily kept pace with the others. They reached Camp 1 in about four hours. Half a dozen sites populated the space, but not the one they were expecting. Erica and Jim were nowhere to be found.

The twins went slack jawed. "Unbelievable," Kathy said.

*Not really*, Norma Jean thought. She and Susan avoided each other's eyes.

After a short pause, Susan suggested they make camp. They cleared a site for the two tents and walled it off from the wind.

"Let's switch partners so we can get to know one another better," Susan said. With that, Carol rolled her sleeping bag out in Norma Jean's tent and Susan joined Kathy.

"Better start dinner," Norma Jean said. She scraped her mitten across a snow shelf to smooth it out and then unpacked her stove, fuel bottle, and pouch of dehydrated beef and chili mac.

"I'll man the stove if you guys get the snow."

Susan placed her food packet next to Norma Jean's. She passed through the break in the wall, then turned to Carol and Kathy.

"Coming?"

The twins blushed in precisely the same shade of red.

"Um," Kathy said, "we've packed our food a little differently from how you do it."

"What do you mean?"

"The idea was to do cooperative cooking. Carol and I have the flour, rice, cheese, and sugar. Erica has some other ingredients. And the pressure cooker."

Susan paused. "Oh. You didn't pre-assemble your meals, then."

"Right."

Susan tapped her lips with her mittened fingers. "Hmm."

Norma Jean tried to absorb the startling news. She had some extra food for storm days and emergencies. She dug through her pack and pulled out two more chili macs.

"Here," she said.

The twins' red cheeks deepened to burgundy, and they accepted the food with whispered thanks.

The awkwardness faded as they ate, and soon they were all talking and laughing like lifelong pals. Susan retold the same stories she'd shared the night before. Norma Jean pulled out her prized Toblerone bar and passed bits of chocolate around. Twilight surrounded them, and the shadows deepened. Their voices rang out in the still air.

Thoughts of Grant and Dave intruded now and then. Mostly Norma Jean was able to keep them tucked away, yet guilt hummed just below the surface. By being on this expedition, she would miss the memorial services.

Carol and Kathy launched into a story about switching places in elementary school. Norma Jean wasn't sure what was more amusing: the tale itself or the way they volleyed back and forth, building on each other's descriptions and making everything more elaborate as they went.

She laughed with Susan, but the feeling made her physically uncomfortable. It dredged up tears that were impossible to hold back. She blinked and stood up.

"I need to go to bed."

Susan gave her a concerned look. She nodded and said goodnight. Soon the others followed. As they settled in, someone skied into the campsite and quietly stepped out of their bindings. Boots crunched and scraped the ice underfoot. Norma Jean and Carol sat up and crawled out of their tent at the same time as Susan and Kathy.

There stood a woman with unruly brown hair and a man with a weathered face. The woman's smile did not reach her eyes.

"We found you," she said.

Carol and Kathy rushed her and threw their arms around her.

"Erica, what happened to you?"

"Where have you been?"

"You have the food, right? And the pressure cooker?"

Like a stern mother, Erica held up a finger to hush the twins.

"Let's get into your tent, Kathy," she said. "Then we'll talk."

Kathy pulled back the tent flap, and Erica crawled in first. Then the twins and Susan. Norma Jean started in, but Jim cut in front of her and took up the remaining space. Norma Jean tied back the flap and knelt just outside. She hugged herself for warmth and longed to be back in her sleeping bag.

Erica introduced herself and Jim to the Alaskans. Her manner was formal and commanding, as though she was a real expedition leader who had lived up to her responsibilities.

She directed her words at Susan.

"You know," she began, "when we arrived in Talkeetna, the weather was so perfect, it seemed a shame to waste it at the airstrip."

She turned to Norma Jean.

"We decided to fly in early and get things in order at Base Camp." Here, she paused and beamed at Jim. "But Jim here thought it was too nice of a day to wait, so we all moved right on up to Camp 1."

Norma Jean crossed her arms tighter and stared back at her.

Erica continued.

"And today, when we sent Carol and Kathy back to retrieve you, Jim thought we would make better use of our time by moving camp up to 11,200 feet."

She regarded Susan again. "We were sure you would understand."

No one spoke, and the twins scowled. Everyone stared at Jim. He mumbled something about needing to put up his tent and scrambled outside. Norma Jean didn't take his place. Better to shiver out here in the cold than to imply she was all-in with Erica.

"Well, I don't understand," Carol said. "We're supposed to be working together. You had the stove and pressure cooker and a bunch of the food. How were we supposed to eat?"

Erica opened her mouth, but Kathy interrupted.

"You couldn't have left word with another team?"

Another uncomfortable silence followed.

Susan waited a few beats.

"The important thing is we're all together now," she said with quiet certainty. "From this moment on, we will work as a team."

Here was the expedition's real leader, Norma Jean thought. Everyone exited the tent and hugged each other. Norma Jean and Carol climbed back into their tent, and Norma Jean drifted off feeling more confident than she had since Talkeetna.

A brilliant mid-morning sky met them as they crawled into the open. It was almost possible to track the shadows receding as the sun climbed higher. The hanging glaciers surrounding them twinkled in icy blue-whiteness. Sun-released avalanches rumbled in the distance. Norma Jean could not imagine a more beautiful place. This was where she belonged.

The others had also slept hard, and Susan's cheek was embossed with a zipper print from her sleeping bag. The twins' hair defied gravity, and they teased each other about it. Norma Jean imagined what wild-haired Erica's bedhead must look like. She turned toward the couple's tent.

It was gone.

She stood still and stared. It took a full minute before Susan, Carol, and Kathy noticed. Nobody bothered with words. All the anger and disappointment had been expressed, and it hadn't made any difference.

They broke camp and headed up the glacier hill, two to a rope. Defeated, they moved more slowly than Norma Jean expected.

"Anger is a heavy thing, especially when you are carrying a full backpack," she thought.

Two hours later, a cramp seized her lower abdomen. She breathed carefully, hoping it would fade. Instead, it intensified, surging wider and deeper and forcing her to stop. She ripped off her gloves and gripped the waistband of her climbing pants.

"Gotta stop!" she yelled back at Carol, her ropemate. She took three wide sidesteps off the trail.

The pants came down just in time for the first release. How could something so embarrassing create such relief? She glanced at Carol, thirty feet down rope. She was also crouched, pants at her knees. Norma Jean turned the other way and saw that Kathy and Susan, too, were squatting.

Why this? Why now? Contaminated water? She wished she had been the one to collect the snow for the dinner pot.

Another cramp took over, and it became clear they were going to be a while. At least it wasn't just her.

Their predicament only got worse. A team of men was barreling up toward them. Norma Jean pivoted around to hide her backside, but it hardly mattered. They trotted along the well-marked trail, coming within a couple of feet. They didn't avert their eyes or hide their laughter. The scene rolled out in slow motion. Norma Jean tucked her head and prayed she would never see them again.

When they had finally passed, the last one yelled back.

"You see the damnedest things in the mountains!"

There was nothing else to do but clean up and keep moving toward Camp 2. But they felt weak, and it was late when they arrived.

Erica had spotted the team as they neared camp, and she greeted them in full mother-hen mode. Norma Jean was too tired to refuse assistance with her pack. Nor did she turn away the hot chocolate that was proffered. Erica extracted Norma Jean's tent and began erecting it inside an already-built camp. The only appropriate response was to join in.

The twins took out Carol's tent, but their efforts to put it up were slow and clumsy. Erica took over, piecing the poles together and giving gentle directions.

The hot chocolate gave Norma Jean and Susan enough energy to make their dinner. Norma Jean's gut still felt raw, and she volunteered to gather snow for the pot. Camp 2, also known as 11

Camp for its elevation, was notorious for its hidden crevasses, and she probed her way to a distant edge.

The wind stirred and clouds accumulated as they ate. After dinner, Norma Jean retired. She craved the warmth and comfort of her own space. The others crowded into Erica and Jim's tent to hash things out. The noise level rose with the twins' accusations and fell with Erica's attempted justifications. It was all just static to Norma Jean. She knew she should still be mad, but it was sadness that engulfed her.

Morning arrived under gray and swirling skies. Norma Jean felt lethargic. After an early visit to the latrine, she tunneled in and went back to sleep. The plan was to take a load of gear and food up past Windy Corner at around 13,500 feet, bury it in a cache, and return here to 11 Camp for the night. Tomorrow, they would move everything up to 14 Camp.

A debate outside the tent woke her. She listened and determined that Erica was pushing to go all the way up to 14 Camp today.

"We should rest and acclimate here," argued one of the twins.

"Yeah! And we need more practice working together as a *team*," said the other. "Especially before we hit Windy Corner."

"This is this Jim's idea, isn't it."

Erica ignored the needling.

"We'll be just fine if we stop at 14 Camp," she said. "We'll take extra time to rest once we get there."

"What do you think, Susan?"

"Well," she started, "on the one hand—"

Norma Jean sneezed, and Susan stopped talking.

"You're awake!" Erica said. "Can you come out here? We want to get your opinion."

She dressed and pulled on her hat and mittens. The extra sleep had restored her energy, and as she crawled outside, she began to feel excited. The group's eyes were on her.

Conventional wisdom said to take the ascent slowly and give the body plenty of time to get used to each new elevation. They had moved more quickly than planned. Yet 14,000 feet was a pivotal point on Denali. She thrilled at the thought of reaching it.

"I actually feel pretty good," she said. "If everyone else does, too, then let's do it. There's a group of doctors there doing medical research. It would be a good place to spend our extra days acclimatizing."

Carol and Kathy cocked their heads and looked at Norma Jean in surprise. They nodded.

"Good point," Carol said.

Erica's smile radiated a warmth that Norma Jean had not yet witnessed.

The group broke down the tents, buried their skis in a marked cache, and rebalanced gear between their backpacks and sleds. The steeper the route, the less weight they wanted to tow behind them. They donned crampons and adjusted them for a tight fit against their boots, double checking for loose laces and straps.

Until now, the glacier had seemed endless, broken only by the wrinkles of snow-covered crevasses and edged with towering seracs. Here at 11,200 feet, the route narrowed. Cliffs on either side forced them up an icefall blown clean of snow on Motorcycle Hill. It wasn't a technical section, rather a mental challenge to leave the horizontal snowfield for a semi-vertical ice climb. Suddenly they were irrefutably on the mountain.

The West Buttress route continues winding its way from the top of Motorcycle Hill. It arches up and around Windy Corner and finally to the large plateau at 14,200 feet. Along the way, they steered around dozens of crevasses while the gusts picked up. The infamous corner was scoured to pale blue ice that made their crampons function like thumbtacks on glass. They took their time, belaying each other across tricky crevasse crossings, each cursing loudly at her unruly sled. By the time they crested Windy Corner, they were navigating in near-whiteout conditions.

Jim and Erica, who had gone first on the rope, waited for the team there. Jim yelled over the roar. He jabbed his mittened hand at a partially collapsed crevasse.

"We need to dump our sleds here. And more stuff, or we won't make it."

Norma Jean absorbed his words. They would stash the sleds and extra food and gear in the rift, mark it, and leave it to climb to 14 Camp, where they would sleep. Then, when weather conditions improved, they would come back down to retrieve the food and gear. Any plan for lightening their loads seemed solid to Norma Jean and the others. They tossed items into sacks and planted a wand to mark their cache.

After Windy Corner, they began to feel the effects of their quick ascent. They breathed hard and took baby steps.

At 14 Camp, male climbers and high-altitude research doctors gathered around to behold the Women on Denali Expedition with its plus-one. The massive basin was bustling with people prepping for the upper mountain. Norma Jean knew some personally and others by reputation. Everyone was generous with food and warm beverages.

Norma Jean and her teammates shoveled out an abandoned site and repaired the stacked walls before erecting their tents. Then, through blowing snow, they wandered over to the campsite of a large group from Mountain Travel—the bigwigs of international guiding services. Norma Jean hovered at the edge of the crowd and peeked between heavy down jackets. She strained to hear what was being said. Wind filtered through the guides' voices, and she had to piece together their story.

The previous month, a German couple vacationing in Fairbanks had decided to attempt Denali. They arrived in Talkeetna, rented outerwear and gear, and ignored the concerns of a pilot and a guide who warned them that they were ill-prepared. The man was a strong, overly confident climber, while his partner struggled to keep up. Several people had encountered them on the West Buttress route and near the top. Despite appearing lethargic and asking other climbers for food, they made it to the summit. A guide from another summiting team offered to let them rope in together on the descent, but they refused. The weather was deteriorating, and the guide needed to get his own team to safety, so he left.

Wind battered the upper reaches of Denali that night and all the next day. A guide radioed to Base Camp to report that the couple had not returned to High Camp. After the weather cleared, a pilot circled the summit area and spotted two bodies northwest of a subpeak called Archdeacon's Tower. All these weeks later, the bodies had not yet been recovered and were still in sight of the trail.

Norma Jean squeezed her eyes shut and hugged herself. She longed to go and cocoon in her sleeping bag but couldn't quite fight the urge to be around others. She stomped her feet for warmth. More stories burst forth, all of them involving death.

Her friend Nick Parker, an experienced Denali guide, caught sight of her. Her unseeing stare prompted him to walk over. He looked alarmed.

"I know you just lost your friends on Dan Beard," he observed. "That's so hard."

A response—any response—would have broken her composure. She couldn't have it. She turned and walked to her tent. Wisely, Nick let her go.

From inside her sleeping bag, she could hear the riotous fun the climbers were having. They were passing around their best snacks and sipping sugary drinks. It was the kind of night in which lasting friendships were formed.

Like the one Grant and Dave had.

Somehow she overcame the urge to cry. Tears and a runny nose were messy inconveniences she couldn't afford right now. She slid down and buried herself deeper.

In the morning, the wind died down, but snow and a thick cloud layer blanketed the camp. Erica, Jim, and Kathy offered to go back to Windy Corner and retrieve the team's cached gear, and the others gladly accepted. Norma Jean contented herself by hanging around in camp and reorganizing gear. She finished the day in a fog of reading and drinking tea. When the others returned, they held a team meeting. After a long discussion, they agreed to haul "carry" loads up to 16,000 feet and return to 14 Camp to sleep.

She nodded off to the muffled sounds of arguing.

The next morning, Erica and Jim emerged with bags under their eyes. Tension crackled between them. They bickered as the team roped up. Erica glared at Jim, while Jim pointedly looked the other way. The team climbed without incident on the moderate terrain leading out of camp, but when they arrived at the base of a steep, icy section known as Headwall, the couple's détente fell apart.

Mountaineering rangers for the Park Service had placed fixed lines along Headwall for climbers to clip into. A jumar device will secure a climber to the fixed rope and allow them to move upward without slipping backward. Erica instructed the team to jumar in to the fixed line while simultaneously doing a running belay.

"That's a waste of time," Jim growled. "We don't need both."

Erica stopped tying into her harness and swung her head to face Jim. Dark sunglasses hid her angry eyes.

"I am the team leader," she said quietly. "It's my call."

He batted at the air as if it were a nuisance. "But you're wrong."

"I'm right, and you need to back off now, *Jim*."

He looked at the others, perhaps hoping to get some support. Norma Jean didn't have a lot of experience in this sort of thing, but surely more safety was better than less. She slowly shook her head at Jim.

His voice rose.

"You are a stubborn woman," he shouted at Erica. "When do you ever listen to reason?"

Now it was her voice that echoed around the cirque.

"I've had it with you," she screamed. "Bastard!"

She ripped off the rope attached to her harness—about 11 pounds of it—and flung it down the steep slope into Jim. He stumbled backward but caught himself. Stunned and slack-jawed, he stared up at Erica.

"What a joke," he muttered.

He detached his rope from the upward-bound line and sidestepped to the other, hooking himself in and beginning his descent. Later, they learned he had made it back to Base Camp.

The Women on Denali Expedition continued up the mountain with double protection. No one spoke, except when necessary. A guided team was on its way down, and the leader paused to for a friendly exchange. He began talking about the German pair who had died near the summit.

He said, "You won't believe it! They are right on the trail! I don't know how they died or what happened to them, but you have to step right over them!"

The other women expressed their horror at hearing this, but Norma Jean froze, unable to speak. The words rolled around and around her head. "You have to step right over them."

As they continued the ascent, she shut out the words and moved with robotic precision. She helped install the team's cache inside an old snow cave at 16,000 feet. They descended rapidly and with ease back to 14 Camp.

That evening was euphoric for the other women, and Norma Jean briefly got caught up in it. The summit seemed within reach. They felt strong and healthy. Now if only the weather would hold.

At bedtime, though, Norma Jean's excitement leached away and her dread flooded back in. Closing her eyes summoned images of Grant and Dave. She imagined stepping over *them* as she struggled for the summit. Death was everywhere in the mountains, an unavoidable presence. It waited up higher in the form of hypothermia, altitude sickness, avalanches, and missed footsteps.

She hunkered down in her sleeping bag but couldn't drive out the cold. She wanted the hell out of there. She wanted off the mountain. When she could no longer stand it, she put on her camp booties and walked over to Nick Parker's site.

"I need to go down," she said.

"What?" he said. "Why?"

"It's just ... everything."

"Norma Jean," he said soothingly, wrapping his big, parka-clad arms around her. "You've worked so hard and you've made it so far."

She pulled back and shook her head. "I don't care."

"What brought you to this decision?"

She considered not telling him, not giving him another way to try to talk her out of it. But she relented.

"The German climbers. Near the summit."

"Ohhhh," he said. "I get it. Yeah, that's pretty awful. But people like to make big stories out of bad stuff. Passing those bodies is just one moment, just one tiny part of climbing this mountain."

She closed her mouth and her eyes.

"I think those boys you climbed with, they would have wanted you …"

He drifted off.

She looked back up at him. "I need to go down. Now."

His eyes were misty when he met hers. He nodded.

Norma Jean spent the rest of the night packing and separating her gear from her teammates'. She would leave them the tent, of course, and anything else they might need to borrow. In the early morning, she pulled them together to explain. None of the other Women on Denali members argued with her decision, but it seemed that Susan was the only one who truly understood. A broken soul could not carry you to the top of a mountain. She needed time to heal.

She took Norma Jean's hands in hers and wished her a safe journey.

Norma Jean roped on as the last member of Nick Parker's descending group. The mountain was no less beautiful on the downward journey. She spotted features on rock faces and saw views that she had been too exhausted to notice while climbing up. She knew she would come back to the mountain. She knew it would be there for her. Just as she had as a 16-year-old aspiring climber, she knew her time would come.

## CHAPTER 6
# Sharpening Skills

**1980-1985**

The thrill of the climb only grew in Norma Jean. Being on a mountain was like living inside a painting. You were part of the panorama, with nothing separating you from the snow and ice and rock and sky. You felt the view with all your senses and reveled in the beauty. In challenging moments, the mountain sowed cold into your hands and feet, while the wind siphoned your body of warmth. Climbing forced intense concentration on your immediate surroundings as, one movement at a time, you pushed your body beyond all predefined limits.

The ascent was so intoxicating to Norma Jean, it even overpowered the trauma that lingered after Grant and Dave's deaths.

In the summer of 1980, she accompanied the Harvard men to the Delta Mountains at the easternmost point of the Alaska Range. They spent most of the season there in the comparatively lower elevations. Then they moved on to Washington's Mt. Rainier. Although her alpine proficiency had improved since her first days on the Ruth Glacier, she still had a long way to go.

"You need rope skills," the Harvard men told her. "You need rock-climbing experience."

Yosemite was the very best place to learn, they assured her. Although it felt like a bold move to go alone, she dipped into her savings and traveled there in the fall of 1980. After spending a night at Geoff's family's house outside Yosemite National Park, she drove in and set herself up in the Sunnyside Walk-in

Campground—known in the climbing world as Camp 4. There, she observed some of the world's most influential and innovative rock jocks and studied their techniques. Life felt awkward, though, before she found a partner.

Then she met Leona. A well-seasoned rock climber, the only thing Leona lacked was experience as a lead. Norma Jean was happy to be her second on the rope. They started on the most basic routes, with Leona coaching Norma Jean on anchoring and belaying. The tutelage continued for much of the fall. Norma Jean returned to Yosemite in 1981.

She undertook a long expedition on the Ruth Glacier in the spring of 1982 with friends from work. The group explored the glacier's west fork, which is known for more variable, sometimes unreliable rock and taller peaks. A highlight was climbing the Ruth Gap—a ridge separating the Ruth and Kahiltna Glaciers—and looking down on Denali's base camp.

That summer, she gained more rock-climbing exposure on trips to England, Wales, and Europe. She funded her passion in part by continuing to work as a sales associate at REI and other sport retailers in the off seasons. REI prioritized outdoor expertise in its salesforce and gladly employed her when she was available.

In 1983, she began working each May and June on the Ruth Glacier as an instructor for the professional guiding service Genet Expeditions. Her job was to prepare novice clients for the rigors of Denali. She taught them mountaineering skills—everything from winter camping to crevasse avoidance and rescue—while keeping them safe from the glacier's hazards. Training others to climb Denali sharpened her own skills and increased her confidence. Nearly all her students were men, bigger and stronger than she, and some brought along their condescending attitudes.

One guy arrived in camp and unloaded his backcountry skis from the bush plane.

"Little girl," he said, looking her up and down. "I could ski your ass into the ground."

She laughed and shot back, "My job is to keep *your* ass out of a crevasse."

Eventually, Norma Jean's expertise earned her a promotion at Genet Expeditions and a move from the Ruth Glacier to Kahiltna Base Camp on Denali. Her new position as an assistant guide meant—in addition to making sure clients were well fed and relatively comfortable—she would help lead them up the mountain. But the "assistant" part of the job ensured that, if a climber suffered from altitude sickness, hypothermia, frostbite, injury, or fear, she would be the one to care for him instead of proceeding to the summit with the rest of the team.

As one of the few women on the mountain, she was always receiving well-meaning assistance from the men. This caused her to question her own capabilities. Once, she worked with a guide named John Svenson for an outfitter other than Genet. There were eight burly firefighters on the expedition, and someone was always swooping in to help her.

"Let me carry that for you."

"I'll start the stove."

"I brushed off your tent."

There had also been a lone climber tacked onto the expedition. He arrived at Base Camp unknown to anyone, firefighters and guides, alike. His crampons were still in the packaging, and they later discovered he had two dozen pairs of cotton underwear in his pack. He made it as far as 14 Camp. Norma Jean was tasked with supervising him, while the team headed for the summit. The man, it turned out, was on a suicide mission. He attempted to hurl himself off a place called The Edge of the World that overlooked a six-thousand-foot drop. Norma Jean and the park rangers held him back.

The experience shook her. It forced her to assess her place as a climber. As an assistant guide, she was forever being saddled with climbers incapable of reaching the summit, and she might never reach it. As a woman, she couldn't manage to free herself of oversolicitous men. Never mind being a team *leader*, she wasn't even sure she was an effective team *member*.

Norma Jean wasn't the type to sit and obsess over a problem. In 1985, she began talking to people in the climbing community, laying out the issue, and seeking their opinions. The response from two friends was both a surprise and a spur to action. It would cause her to make a choice that would change her life.

Their advice? Climb alone.

## CHAPTER 7
# Team of One

**1985-1986**

It was a couple of Daves who urged Norma Jean to climb by herself.

Dave Johnston was a Denali State Park Ranger, legendary mountaineer, and a valued friend who had been a member of the first team to summit the mountain in winter. He was known for his calm, logical approach to climbing. She prized his advice.

"When you climb alone," he counseled, "you will learn so much about yourself."

Alone. The word rang out. Her mind went still, and her eyes widened.

Johnston smiled and nodded.

"I know, I know. But it's the only way to evaluate your own abilities. Just try."

Later she approached her friend Dave Staeheli, a guide she had worked with at Genet Expeditions and an accomplished mountaineer.

"You are perfectly capable of soloing," he said. "Go up there and prove to yourself what you can do."

She began laying the plans.

In the summer and fall of 1985, she hiked up the slopes around Palmer and Anchorage with a heavy pack. She rock-climbed on weekends and evenings. When time ran short, she squeezed in a run or a bike ride or a weight-set at the gym. Winter meant ice-climbing and skiing the Chugach backcountry.

She continued working at REI for most of the year. As new merchandise arrived in the store—lighter-weight sleeping pads; underlayers in the latest synthetic fabric; boot liners made of fast-drying foam—she wanted to buy it all. Better gear meant a better chance at making the top. However, this brought on a different sort of danger: the one that comes from spending your whole paycheck at your workplace. She compensated by getting as much overtime as she could.

Her mother, Jean Marsh, didn't care about all these practicalities. Her only concern was the terrifying possibility of losing Norma Jean. In February 1984, world-famous adventurer Naomi Uemura had disappeared after completing the first wintertime solo ascent of Denali. He reached the summit, began his descent, and reported his position to a pilot who was flying nearby. Then Uemura vanished. If the mountain could claim a 43-year-old alpinist with over two decades of experience, how could Jean be sure the same wouldn't befall her only daughter?

She fretted about a story Norma Jean had told her after returning from a guiding trip with Genet Expeditions, the same year Uemura disappeared. She was helping lead a group of women up the Kahiltna. They were on skis and towing heavy sleds. In the distance, they saw the colorful specks of descending climbers. She felt giddy as she imagined asking them about conditions up higher on the peak, crevasse dangers, and how long it took them to summit—assuming they had made it.

As the group neared, the colorful specks evolved into pink and teal parkas and pants, not the usual red, blue, green and rust of American fabrics. The leader stopped right beside Norma Jean. He shook his head in wonder and batted a hand at her harness.

"What is that you are wearing?" he said in a French accent.

"It's a harness," she answered. "We rope together on the glacier for safety."

He tossed his head back and laughed. "You Americans! You travel like turtles!"

The seventeen-member group skied past, and sure enough, no one was roped together.

"Enjoy your burden!" the leader yelled back.

Norma Jean let them pass.

"Of course we rope up," she said to her team. "We're not idiots."

"No," chuckled one of the women. "We're turtles!"

She turned and shook a fist at the receding team.

"Tortue!" she yelled in French.

"Schildkröte!" yelled another woman in German.

"Tortuga!" Norma Jean added in hastily remembered, high-school Spanish.

"Honu!" someone else hollered in Hawaiian.

Their laughter took the sting out of the insult, and each passing crevasse affirmed their choice.

The next day, they were acclimating at 11 Camp with the rest of their group when they heard some horrifying news. A Swiss team had lost their leader in a crevasse on the Kahiltna. The more they learned, the more it became obvious it was the guy who had taunted them for roping together.

"They rounded the corner near the East Fork, near the airstrip," someone said. "The team had one rope, and it was in the leader's pack."

• • •

"You won't be roped to anyone, either," her mother said. "How can you assure me you won't end up dead in the bottom of a crevasse?"

At first, Norma Jean didn't have an answer. It was harder for a solitary climber to stay safe on the glacier. There were just no guarantees. The best she could promise was to keep in sight of others at all times.

Dave Johnston had a solution: a crevasse self-rescue device he had built for solo climbing. The device included a pair of 20-foot aluminum poles that positioned the climber at the center, like a gymnast on a set of parallel bars. If a climber dropped into a crevasse, the poles were supposed to form a bridge over the hole and allow her to climb out. Johnston named the device Bridgit, a play on the words, "bridge it."

Knowing Norma Jean would use Bridgit helped alleviate some of her mother's fears.

Finally, in mid-May 1986, 27-year-old Norma Jean was ready to start her ascent. Her gear had been pared back to the essentials, and pilot Doug Geeting loaded it into the back of his Cessna, along with her sled and skis. He tucked the bag carrying Bridgit's pole segments, wires, and other parts between two piles. Norma Jean tapped her pocket to make sure she had the screws and wingnuts that would hold together the self-rescue device when she reassembled it.

"That Bridgit is a weird contraption," Geeting observed.

She nodded.

"But," he added, "if it can keep Mr. Six-Foot-Seven out of the crevasses, it ought to work for you."

She laughed. "Let's hope I never have to find out."

As they sped along the runway in Talkeetna, engine warbling, she felt the familiar sensations in her stomach. It didn't matter how many times she had been on Denali; the butterflies always returned. The plane lifted, gaining elevation quickly. Below, kettle ponds and rivers punctuated a world of green. The view transitioned to black and white as they passed over rock and ice. The afternoon was clear and the mountain soon dominated the view through Geeting's windshield.

Norma Jean was all nerves. Her mouth had gone dry, but her mind was giddy. A joke simmered. She gritted her teeth for a time, but finally she could no longer stand the tension. The joke had to come out.

"This seemed like such a good idea back at the house!" she giggled.

The pilot chuckled and shook his head.

"I have every confidence in you."

The 44-mile-long Kahiltna Glacier was beneath them, and the hourlong flight passed quickly. Geeting set the plane down on its wheel skis and taxied in a wide U-turn. He stopped next to another plane. Just a hundred yards away from the airstrip, clumps of colorful tents marked Base Camp.

Geeting unloaded the gear, made a visual inspection of the plane, and returned to the cockpit. Norma Jean shuttled everything to the edge of the tent city. She checked in with the camp manager and affirmed her plans to follow the West Buttress route. Although 80 to 90 percent of climbers headed up the same way, plenty of others chose more technical paths to the summit, such as the Cassin Ridge or West Rib. Still others would tackle nearby mountains such as Hunter, Foraker, or Crosson.

Which teams might she keep running into on the West Buttress? As their itineraries synched up, they would learn each other's names, climbing styles, strengths and weaknesses, and camp stories. Nicknames would be awarded. She had collected several over the years as an assistant guide.

Her campsite had been vacated recently by other climbers. Its footprint was already dug out, and the snow blocks were cut and stacked. The place was dotted with tobacco spit, food spills, and bits of trash. She spent an hour hatcheting out the detritus and leveling the floor. Setting up her tent was the easy part. She had brought her one-person bicycle-touring tent that was just big enough for her body and a small complement of gear. Not only was it lightweight and compact inside her backpack, its simple design made it easy to put up. An A+ shelter if there ever was one.

It would take the rest of the day to sort her gear and assign it a spot in her backpack, on her sled, or in the cache she had dug nearby. She buried the gear in the cache and marked it with a long red wand with a tiny flag. Afterward, she stopped by the neighboring campsites, introducing herself and sharing a hot drink here and a handful of trail mix there. Then, reluctantly, she returned to her own site and prepared two packs of spaghetti. She ate them alone.

She turned in for the night. Quarters were tight inside the bicycle touring tent. Maybe it didn't exactly deserve an A+, at least not for mountaineering. It was unimportant now, though. Sleep was all that mattered. Dawn would arrive soon enough.

At 4 a.m., she awoke to the green glow of the tent and the sounds of camp coming alive. Stoves hissed, boots crunched on snow, carabiners clinked. She made a quick breakfast of oatmeal and instant coffee and then packed up the last of her gear. In all her years on Denali, she had never left Base Camp alone. There was always some client whose backpack straps needed tightening or whose sled was off balance, some friend to lend words of encouragement. The teams around her this morning were in varying stages of readiness, from those still sacked out in their tents to others who were already skiing toward the trail.

Norma Jean laid out her climbing kit just so. She attached her sled to the tail end of Bridgit, then hoisted on her backpack. She stepped into the middle of the contraption and fastened the connecting bar to her harness at hip level. The twenty-foot poles jutted out way ahead and behind her. She clicked into the bindings of her skis and took up her ski poles.

Wearing Bridgit made her self-conscious. No one here would have a clue what it was. It just looked weird. She skied out of Base Camp, chin up, face forward, poles pointing the way.

On the West Buttress route, a mountaineer has to go down before she can go up. Norma Jean descended the steep half mile down Heartbreak Hill to 6,800 feet before rising slowly over five and a half miles to Camp 1. The snow-covered Kahiltna was wide and open, and the trail led her far from the avalanche-prone slopes surrounding it. She skied along with eyes always on the lookout for crevasses. Even the best-traveled path could give way unexpectedly. You never fully knew whether you were skiing over ice or air.

Norma Jean was taking on Denali expedition style, like everyone else she knew. It was a multi-step approach designed to help climbers acclimate on the ascent. After establishing camp at one place, she would drop a partial load of gear at a higher elevation and then return to the lower camp to sleep.

In Camp 1, it snowed heavily overnight, and Norma Jean began to grasp the limitations of her bicycle-touring tent. As the snow accumulated, the tent sagged and threatened her already-limited headroom. The waterproof fabric trapped moisture from her breath, and water droplets clung to the walls. Every hour, she slipped out the entrance and shoveled snow off the top.

The next day, as she skied out of camp, the wind invited Bridgit to play. It started with a mild breeze that nudged the parallel bars upward. Norma Jean stopped to regain her balance and wait for the air to still. This happened a handful of times until she got used to it. She skied another mile across the glacier, following the trail as it meandered around the deadly pockmarks that signified crevasses. Then the wind came at her crosswise, yanked one pole upward, and almost tipped her onto her side. Next, it spun her 180 degrees. Norma Jean's annoyance was tinged with fear. If she fell down, her 60-pound pack went with her, and all that weight slamming to the ground might open up a hole underneath. At such an odd angle, Bridgit would not be in a position to arrest her fall.

How she missed having people to commiserate with. Was anyone watching now? Maybe they were snickering as Bridgit tried to spin like a satellite. It was humiliating to think about, but also kind of funny.

Bridgit had proved herself useful in Camp 1 and later at Camp 2, (11 Camp), as a drying rack. Each morning, Norma Jean draped her damp sleeping bag across the parallel poles. In minutes, the moisture froze into tiny, white granules that she simply whisked off the fabric. Crevasses riddled 11 Camp and its surroundings, and Norma Jean knew she should continue wearing the device. But when she prepared to move up the mountain, she couldn't stand to put it on again. She buried it and marked the spot for retrieval on the descent.

Windy Corner's legendary gusts were manageable, and she stopped long enough to take a self-portrait. A bandana and glacier glasses protected her face from the sun. Above the bend, at around 13,500 feet, a collapsed snow cornice over a shallow crevasse made the perfect place for another cache. She stowed her skis, donned her boots, and strapped on her crampons.

A short distance beyond the cache, she came to an open crevasse. A glance into its blackness told her it was deep. Without her skis to distribute her weight, she was more vulnerable to puncturing the thin-crusted edges and falling in.

"What timing," she muttered.

She took a few breaths, praying the surface around it wouldn't give way, and lunged across. Her sled clattered behind her, and she skittered up a few steps to pull it clear of the rift.

Good fortune continued to accompany her up the mountain. The weather at 14 Camp stayed clear and relatively calm. The site was prone to storms barreling through, yet conditions were almost always better than those at higher elevations.

Fourteen Camp offered something else that added peace of mind for a lone traveler. The Park Service had established an outpost there, staffed with climbing rangers who could assist in rescues and take care of those who were injured or sick. Nearby, visiting doctors conducted research on the effects of cold and altitude on climbers who volunteered to be part of a study. Thus, 14 Camp had earned the nickname Medical Camp.

Norma Jean planned a four-night stay to rest and adjust to the elevation. She felt lucky that she didn't seem to be susceptible to altitude sickness, but then again, she was usually careful not to ascend too quickly. Now she spent the days with others enjoying views of 14,573-foot Mt. Hunter with its spiny, iguana-like ridge and the wide body of 17,402-foot Mt. Foraker. A sun-charged optimism pervaded the place.

She left her sled and continued climbing expedition style until she reached High Camp at 17,200 feet. The double-carrying method was slow and plodding. A person was essentially climbing the mountain twice. But here the double-carrying would stop.

She set up camp and spent a couple of nights acclimating and sorting her gear. One morning, she paused to fulfill a promise. Anchorage musician and comedy club owner Douglas Haggar—better known as "Mr. Whitekeys"—had agreed to finance her flights in and out of Base Camp on one condition: She had to haul a can of Hormel SPAM along and take a picture of herself with it on the mountain.

With her boot liners hanging up to dry behind her, Norma Jean swapped her warm hat for a "Fly by Night Club" ballcap. Another climber snapped the picture. Tanned and relaxed, she hugged her knees and smiled. The bright sky seemed to promise a smooth path ahead.

It was day 13. She streamlined her pack, leaving everything behind that wasn't essential to a 12-hour, round-trip push to the summit. In case she got caught in a storm or needed to warm up, she carried a sleeping bag and a waterproof outer layer called a bivvy bag. She packed snacks for lunch and dinner, two bottles of water, prewarmed against the cold, and all her regular climbing equipment.

She wore her heaviest ensemble: vapor-barrier socks, boot liners, boots, and gaiters on her feet, polypropylene and fleece layers in the middle and her down parka on top. A pile hat swaddled her head and a balaclava was tucked into a pocket. Enormous summit mittens covered thick gloves and liners.

She collapsed her tent and weighed it down with extra gear. A team of three men was breaking down their camp nearby.

• • •

She ascended the Autobahn, where the trail made an upward arc from High Camp at 17,200 feet to Denali Pass a thousand feet higher. The path was no wider than a pair of boots, and a misstep would be disastrous. There was a grim reason the area was nicknamed the "Autobahn."

After Denali Pass, Norma Jean reached a quarter-mile-long plateau known as the Football Field. Although it was a comparatively flat stretch, the 19,500-foot elevation made it a slog. The wind picked up during the half hour it took her to plod across. The summit ridge ahead and above was growing fuzzy, its edge becoming duller under the billowing snow. Then it disappeared in a cloud.

She stopped and waited. Perhaps the cloud would get swept away. Instead, the scene grew worse.

The three-man team from High Camp caught up and passed her.

"Keep going!" one of them called.

Were they not seeing what she was?

An internal voice nagged at her. Its tone was familiar and demanding, and it sounded like Mother. How could she keep going if she couldn't see? Staying put wasn't safe, either. Year after year, climbers had gotten stranded on the Football Field. Some had headed the wrong way and fallen to their deaths.

A gust of wind rushed in and broadsided her. It was so much colder and so much harder to defy than anything she had faced before. Head down, she leaned in and pressed on. The wind reared up again just a few steps later and smacked her. She fell, hands and knees busting through crusty snow.

No, no, no, no. With just Pig Hill and the summit ridge ahead, a mere 90 minutes lay between her and the top. She forced herself to her feet and started walking again, but the final blast was violent. Norma Jean crashed onto her side and rolled to her back. She would have to retreat.

## CHAPTER 8
# A Hair's Breadth

She began retracing her steps toward the Football Field. Angry tears soaked her balaclava and froze it to her face. She had started this climb for herself, but along the way a whole host of people had begun following her movements and waiting to learn that she had summited: Her parents and brothers, friends and coworkers from REI and Genet Expeditions, Denali climbing rangers, her partner and his friends, and even Mr. Whitekeys, who planned to announce her success to his nightclub patrons. How could she face them after coming so very, very close to the top—and failing?

Without thinking, she pivoted and started back up toward the summit ridge; airborne snow had blotted it out. Continuing on would be suicide. She stood wide, balled her fists, and hollered into the wind.

Hours later, she reached the Autobahn, the last steep segment between her and High Camp somewhere below. Her body was depleted, and her legs quivered. She faced outward and began heel plunging, one slow step at a time. Clouds hid the camp, but she could sense it down there beckoning to her. The distant oasis gave her hope. Perhaps she could spend a night or two, wait for the wind to die down, and try for the top again. She held her ice axe just under the blade with the spike end pointed into the snow for stability. Her summit mittens made it hard to keep a firm grip.

Then she missed a step.

She let go of the axe as she fell sideways and began sliding headfirst. A thousand feet of icy slope yawned beneath her. She accelerated down the rugged surface, scrambling for a catch-hold. Her nylon parka and climbing pants made a sissing noise as she slid. The axe bounced along at the end of her wrist sling.

Then somehow she crashed, hands first, into a rock. She reared up to avoid smashing her face. Holding still, she let her breath catch up and tried not to panic. Cold seeped into her palms where her mittens had ripped.

She sank down behind the rock, giving in to the weight of her backpack. Her legs still pointed uphill. She considered getting onto hands and knees, but one wrong move could tip her over onto the slope again. Ice ridges and rocks would break her body and toss her like a ragdoll. She might even land in a crevasse. Her stomach felt hot, and her head pounded. She squeezed her eyes shut.

"You're okay."

It was a man's voice, gentle and concerned.

"I need you to sit up."

She opened her eyes, stared at the rock and blinked, not daring to look. What was going on? Had she hit her head? Was she hearing voices now? Strangely, though, she felt obligated to answer.

"I can't!" she cried. "I'm off balance."

A hand reached down. It was covered in an old-fashioned, Norwegian-style wool mitten. It smelled of lanolin. She grabbed it and—reassured by its firm grip—crawled to her knees and rolled into a sitting position. She rested her boots on the rock.

"Thank you."

No one answered. The kind man with the wool mittens had evaporated.

"Shit," she said. "I'm hallucinating."

After checking her boots to make sure her crampons were firmly attached, she climbed back to the trail. She continued the descent, mindful of every footfall.

A tailwind nudged her into High Camp. The three-man team from the Football Field had somehow arrived first. They returned her wave and continued tying down their tent. Norma Jean wanted to get closer, to talk and compare notes, but first she needed to replace her balaclava, which had frozen to her cheeks. She removed her torn mitten and slid her fingers between the mask and her face. The wool stripped away from her skin like a Band Aid. She shoved the balaclava into a pocket and forced the mitten on over her glove again. Her fingers throbbed from the cold.

She longed to commiserate with the other climbers, to offer sympathy and receive theirs. Just imagining the conversation made a lump form in her throat, but before she could collect herself, the trio ducked back into their tent. The shelter quivered in the wind.

It would be rude to go knocking when they probably just needed sleep. She could pay them a visit later. Anyway, her own campsite had degraded over the past 12 hours and required her attention. She pulled her tent out from under the pile of gear weighting it down. She pitched the tent, stretching out the guy lines and hammering the stakes into the hard snow. Then she checked and rechecked that they were secure.

Now, for some ramen. But at over 17,000 feet, the simple act of boiling water could tax her patience. Wind and cold robbed the stove of some of its heat, and filling an empty stomach could take forever. Her last meal had been breakfast, a lifetime ago when she still held hope of summiting. In frustration, she tossed her food bag at the tent. It landed just inside.

When she at last ate, the food went down haltingly and sat like a pile of rocks in her stomach. The storm worsened. The wind punched holes between the snow blocks in her perimeter wall and shaved off the tops. Wanting to burrow into her tent, she instead grabbed her saw and trudged around the camp until she found a patch of snow soft enough to carve. In the end, though, she could only add a single row of blocks to the top. This would have to do. Snow blew in from all sides in the gloomy light.

It was no warmer in the tent, and she kept her hat, parka, overpants, and down booties on as she zipped herself into the sleeping bag. The tent walls rattled and snapped under the wind's assault, while hanging bits of gear trembled on their carabiners. She drifted off, but the racket woke her every few seconds. Anxieties past, present, and future toyed with her mind. She replayed her fall on the Autobahn and relived the rapid acceleration that—if not for a random rock—would have led to her death. Also, of course, the vision or head-trip or illusion of the man who had offered a hand. How was she even supposed to process that?

Regardless, she felt grateful. Even though the man was just her mind playing tricks on her, she had hallucinated the right thing at the right time. At least when she had reached to accept his hand, she didn't lean the wrong way and topple into the abyss.

The storm's roar dredged up more immediate worries. Her tent was better-designed for bicycle tours than mountaineering expeditions. How much pressure could it take? How much longer before the wind split the rubbery fabric and then tore it to shreds? What would she do if—when?—it happened?

The notion overwhelmed her. She tucked her head into her sleeping bag and shut her eyes. Strange how the wind made such scary noises, howling and moaning like lost souls. Underneath the din, she thought she heard men yelling.

Then a gap opened in the tent. She sat up and began thrashing her way out of the sleeping bag. A man's face appeared, and she realized he had simply unzipped the entrance. He beckoned with his mitten. As she came close, he yelled, "We're digging snow caves!"

She bundled up and unstrapped her avalanche shovel from her pack. Leaving the tent meant she risked losing it to the wind. She checked that the stakes and guy lines were holding firm and followed the climber to a narrow ridge that was bulked up with snow. He left her and joined his team to dig as she began excavating her own shelter. Mercifully, her years as a climbing instructor on the Ruth Glacier had prepared her.

The others had chosen a good spot. Much of the snow at High Camp was too icy or compacted to give way to a shovel, but here, the wind had deposited it in a long drift. Norma Jean wondered if the men would shelter together or build individual caves.

She cleared an entryway and began tunneling into the drift. Two feet in, she angled upward and carved out a wider chamber. She opened her parka and stuffed her hat into her pocket to avoid sweating. The cave wasn't her best work and lacked the smooth surfaces and finishing touches of those she had built on the Ruth. It was just a basic emergency shelter that wouldn't shred in the wind.

When it was finished, she returned to the tent. A loose guy line thrashed in the wind. As she crawled inside, the tent inflated like a balloon and pieces of extra clothing tumbled to the rear. She rezipped quickly and began stuffing everything into her backpack. A corner of the tent rose, and then the entire front reared up. The stakes were coming loose.

Both sleeping pads would be needed as insulation in the cave. She rolled up the foam one and strapped it to the outside of the backpack and deflated the blow-up one enough to fit it inside. Her sleeping bag hogged most of the interior space. She removed the tools and utensils hanging from the ceiling and tucked them into the crannies of the backpack.

The pack felt light as she hauled it and her climbing equipment to the snow cave. She tossed her ropes, harness, axe and other necessities inside and then shoved the backpack in just ahead of her. The entry tunnel snaked down and then up into a bluish cavity. She placed everything around the base of the walls. The space was gouged out unevenly, and she had a hard time keeping her pack from flopping over. She stacked her sleeping pads on the lumpy floor and lay her sleeping bag on top. Then she hurried back outside to wrestle down the tent and pocket the few remaining stakes.

It would be hours before her body warmed the cave. She shivered and got back into her bag. The tent had felt cozy by comparison.

She nodded off and woke sometime later from hunger. Strapping on her headlamp, she rummaged through her pack and found a granola bar and some jerky. She dug deeper, searching for the orange nylon bag containing her dehydrated meals and drink mixes. Where was it? One at a time, she pulled every piece of gear out and set it on her lap. She checked the backpack's inside compartments and even the side pockets but came up empty.

Leaving the sleeping bag, she wormed through the tunnel and poked her head out. Her campsite was barely recognizable. It looked more like a crater. Wind had gnawed away the protective walls, and as expected, the food bag was long gone.

She devoured the jerky and granola bar and was instantly hungry again. If the storm lasted much longer, she would have to go begging. She set up her stove at the entry and melted snow for drinking. The water would soothe her stomach for a while and keep her hydrated and thinking clearly. She filled a water bottle and thermos and kept them warm against her skin as she tried to sleep. The cave shuddered with every blast, raising her fears that it would collapse or disintegrate. She didn't dare leave, not even to pee. For that, she repurposed an empty water bottle.

Hours passed slowly. She broke the boredom and tension with a stretching routine meant to help her get back on her feet after the storm. The howling wind grated on her ears and her nerves. Her stomach growled, rearranging the pain every few minutes. It was time to melt more snow, but her stove wouldn't start. She had run out of fuel. She tipped up the cannister to be sure and shook the spent ones.

Staying hydrated was vital to staying warm and clear-headed. Somehow she was going to have to borrow fuel, but the wind would have to ease up before she could venture outside the cave. She listened for breaks in the roar. Hearing none, she returned to her sleeping bag and waited.

Several catnaps later, she got what she needed: a pause, followed by another. She rushed to get her boots, hat, and gloves on and then crawled into the open. The world was engulfed in clouds, and the air was still blustery. She found the entrance to the other snow cave.

"Knock, knock!" she called on her way in.

Three surprised faces greeted her, bodies smushed together amid ropes and backpacks. The stale air smelled of food and farts and body odor.

"Oh, hey! How are you holding up?"

"Wellllll," she said. "I ran out of fuel. … And food."

There was barely a pause before the men scrambled to action. They began reaching into the backpacks along the walls. She loaded her pockets with foil packs and bags of GORP. In her hand, she carried a precious red fuel bottle. She thanked them repeatedly.

"We've been wondering if you summited," one guy said.

"Oh, no. I wish. But it was quite the trip back down here from the Football Field," she said. "I've been dying to talk to you guys about it."

She wouldn't get to tell her story, not yet. A sound like a locomotive bore down on them, and the snow cave trembled. Recess was over.

• • •

The fluctuating wind began to hurt Norma Jean's ears, as though someone had scoured out the canals with sandpaper. Her eardrums felt raw. Hundreds of false alarms had tricked her into thinking it had abated, but now, two days after she had received the extra food and fuel, the wind paused a handful of times. Then it stopped completely. She sat up, waited, counted in the silence. Relief flooded her ears. The torture had stopped.

Outside the cave it was all bluebird and white. She whooped with joy.

"It's over!"

The others crawled into the open, blinking and stumbling. She hugged them and thanked them profusely for giving her aid. Her legs felt wobbly and her balance was off—byproducts of spending five days in confinement—but it wouldn't take long to get back to normal.

"Let's get out of here," someone said.

Norma Jean packed up as quickly as was humanly possible. Surrounded by the others, she began the long descent, stopping along the way to pick up her sled, skis, cached food, and of course, Bridgit.

She reached the base of Heartbreak Hill, the last steep grade before Base Camp. She had chuckled at the name, explained it to tourists, and sympathized with disappointed clients about it, but she had never *felt* it. Now she looked up at the jumble of pyramids and blocks that made up Mt. Francis and let the sadness course through her.

A stray hair dangled from the ruff on her parka and glinted in the sun. She rested her eyes on it as she skied. A hair's breadth is all that had separated Norma Jean from the top of Denali. She had spent hundreds of hours during the past year—saving money, grilling the experts, planning, training, packing and repacking, and finally climbing—and it all came down to the very last, unsurmountable, 90-minute segment. She reached 19,500 feet on North America's highest mountain by herself, yet in the official record, her solo expedition would be defined as a failure.

## CHAPTER 9
# Greater Heights

**Summer 1986**

Norma Jean could not ignore the contradiction: She had turned back from Denali's summit for fear of flying off the mountain. Yet here she was, not two months later, flying off the Chugach Mountains. On purpose. She had taken up paragliding.

Seated in her harness, weightless, she saw the earth drop away in her periphery. Astonishment turned to joy as the wind carried her up into the wide open and then even higher. The whoosh was as constant as a spring stream. She adjusted the brake toggles to keep light pressure on her wing. Flying required full concentration: watching for changes in topography, monitoring her surroundings for hazards, listening.

She had lucked into the opportunity. Having taken an office job at the Genet Expeditions headquarters in Wasilla, she was in the right place at the right time when owners Harry and Diane Johnson acquired the first paragliding equipment in the state. The hang-gliding community had been around since the early 1970s, and the pilots watched their upright-sitting counterparts with curiosity and enthusiasm.

Norma Jean's flights became therapeutic. In the air, she shed the anxieties of a relationship that had disintegrated upon her return from Denali. Her partner, she learned, was not the person she understood him to be. His reckless habits threatened them both, and she left the relationship for her own well-being. Gliding allowed her to shut out the background buzz of anger and betrayal and grief threatening to overwhelm her. Her peace stretched into other areas of life. With a clear mind she could reflect on the Denali trip. Images of immense icefalls, unending peaks, pristine snow, and pastel skies played on a loop in her mind.

Although her doubts intruded every so often, she knew that turning back on Denali's Football Field had been the right decision. She hadn't forgotten the terror of rocketing down the Autobahn headfirst or the dreary tension of sheltering in a snow cave.

Stories in the Anchorage Daily News lauded her summit attempt, bringing her to the attention of Alaskans outside the mountaineering community. The first story reported her painful decision to return as "sane" and a choice "between life and the growing threat of death." The second, a profile that described her as a mountaineer and Mt. McKinley guide, stated that when she got within 600 vertical feet of the summit, high winds and cold drove her down. Both pieces made clear the impossibility of reaching the top.

But it was the song written and performed by her SPAM-loving benefactor, Mr. Whitekeys, that lifted her into the ranks of Alaska folk heroes—and set the stage for another summit attempt.

• • •

At the end of the summer, she returned to her job at REI. Her time in the spotlight had boosted her status, and management delighted in having her back. Customers recognized her from the paper. While she was just another assistant guide at Genet, she was lauded as a seasoned mountaineering expert at REI.

Some of Norma Jean's closest friends worked at the store, and spending time with them felt like coming home. Her friend Lynn was also just returning to the store after working all summer as a rafting guide. She had her own tales but was more interested in Norma Jean's. She asked the best questions. Cindy was enthusiastic and fun. And Katherine, so quiet and unassuming to strangers, had a knack for making her friends snort beer out of their nostrils and nearly pee themselves with laughter.

One night after work, they went to see Mr. Whitekeys and the Spamtones perform at the Fly by Night Club. The women settled in with their drinks. Mr. Whitekeys lambasted Alaska's politicians, poked fun at Anchorage's quirkiness, and celebrated newsworthy locals—all through clever lyrics set to catchy tunes. His performers wore outlandish costumes, and he often sported a top hat, Hawaiian shirt, and mismatched tie.

In the middle of his set, he segued into the song they had been waiting for.

"This one's called 'Norma Jean,'" he said.

"Now it was Norma Jean, yeah Norma Jean
It wasn't Peggy Sue, and it wasn't Sally
It was Norma Jean, yeah Norma Jean
tryin' to be the first solo woman on the top of Mt. Denali

Well it was the ninth of May, that was the fateful day
she first breathed that mountain air kinda' thinly
That glacier pilot flew her in, and then he flew back out again
and there she was at the base of Mt. McKinley

Norma Jean, yeah Norma Jean
crossin' glaciers and crevasses up the valley
Norma Jean, yeah Norma Jean
tryin' to carry a can of Spam to the top of Mt. Denali

Well, the climb it started out OK, but on the third eventful day
she hit those frigid winds that every climber dreads
Yeah it howled and whipped and blew, and before that day was through her tent was ripped and torn into a thousand shreds

And the cold wind kept on blowing, but Norma Jean kept on going
climbin' higher each and every day
And three weeks passed, and at long last, she was makin' progress mighty fast
just 12 climbin' hours, was all that was in the way

Norma Jean, yeah Norma Jean
It wasn't Peggy Sue, and it wasn't Sally
It was Norma Jean, yeah Norma Jean
just twelve climbin' hours from the top of Mt. Denali

Well she started out from 17, and then winds like she'd never seen came roarin' down just like a mad gorilla
The wind it howled and whipped around, it picked her up and set her down and nearly blew her halfway to Wasilla

She dug her ice axe in the snow, and dragged herself a foot or so
She caught her breath, she was at the human limit
There was just 500 feet to go, she could see the top, but the goin's slow
makin' maybe one or two feet per minute

Norma Jean, yeah Norma Jean
tryin' to be the first solo woman on the summit.
Norma Jean, yeah Norma Jean
500 more feet, she woulda' done it

Now when Denali's winds they blow, the mountain takes her toll.
and many's disappeared quick and clean
Some guys froze and then there's those, that only lost a coupla' toes
But that can of Spam protected Norma Jean

It took three weeks up and one day down, and Norma made it back to town
and the record books won't carry Norma's name
And the mountain memory it lingers, but Norma Jean's got all her fingers
and that's the way you win McKinley's game.

Norma Jean, yeah Norma Jean
tryin' to be the first solo woman on the summit
Norma Jean, yeah Norma Jean
If she'd eaten that can of frozen Spam, I think she mighta' done it

(Copyright 1986 by Mr. Whitekeys)

The audience erupted, no one louder than the women from REI. They hugged and bought another round and toasted their teary, beaming friend.

Lynn turned to her, staring earnestly into her eyes and then putting her mouth against her ear so she could hear.

"Oh, my God. You have got to make the summit. You have to."

Norma Jean pulled back and cocked her head. After all the conversations they'd had, how could Lynn—of all people—not understand?

"I tried," she yelled over the noise, adding a shrug for emphasis.

Lynn returned to her ear.

"Not alone. Let us come with you."

## CHAPTER 10
# Rascals

**May 1988**

On Sunday, May 15, 1988, Norma Jean, and her team, REI RascGals ("Rascals" for simplicity), flew into Kahiltna Base Camp on Talkeetna Air Taxi. It would be Lynn, Cindy, and Katherine's first time on the mountain. Their pilot was a familiar face to 29-year-old Norma Jean, someone she had seen around but hadn't yet flown with. As they passed over swaths of cottonwood and spruce, Dan glanced over at her in the passenger seat.

"Did you hear about Lowell's rescue on Friday?" he asked. "Out of Medical Camp?"

Lowell Thomas, Jr. was Dan's boss—a co-owner of Talkeetna Air Taxi and a legend. He flew a turbo-charged Helio Courier airplane and was the only non-helicopter pilot to evacuate climbers from the 14,200-foot camp.

"Uh-uh," Norma Jean said into her microphone. "What happened?"

The plane dipped sharply and came back up. Dan paused to check his instruments, and Norma Jean turned to check on her teammates.

"Whoa!" Katherine said. She stared wide-eyed and then laughed.

Cindy white-knuckled her armrests while her eyes remained glued to the window.

Lynn smiled impassively. To her, the turbulence probably felt no worse than running the rapids on Sixmile Creek.

Dan continued with his story.

"Coupla Chinese climbers made it to the Ridge at 16,000. They had to get out of the weather, so they climbed down the other side a little ways towards Peters Glacier. Both fell into a crevasse but then self-rescued. They got frostbite, of course. It was too windy to put their tent up, so they just wrapped up in it and spent the night that way. One guy couldn't walk in the morning, so the other one dragged himself down to Medical Camp and brought back help."

Dan got on his radio and reported the clear weather to the air taxi's office. He glanced at Norma Jean again.

"They got the guy with the bad feet down to Medical Camp and into the medical tent. They stabilized him, but it took a day and a half for the weather to break. Then Lowell finally made it in there and evac'd both climbers."

This time when Norma Jean turned around, her teammates looked back with nervous expressions.

"Lowell's the best," she said, trying to steer the conversation away from the plight of the climbers.

"Yeah," Dan agreed. "Literally. He's flown the Helio up to 14,000 a dozen times. And yet the man is just as cool as can be. He doesn't even swear."

He shook his head in apparent disbelief.

This was probably true. Over her eight years as a climber flying into and out of Denali National Park, she couldn't recall hearing a single "damn" out of the pilot. His manner was always calm and reassuring, his mood upbeat. He was like an older version of her father.

But Dan wasn't finished with tales of high-altitude rescues.

"I got one that's even better," he said.

"Dan," she said, interrupting. "Dan!"

"What?"

She drew a finger across her throat. Then she tipped her head toward the back of the plane.

"This isn't a good time," she said.

"Gotcha."

After landing, Norma Jean and her Rascals teammates lined up to catch the bags and gear as Dan unloaded the plane. Base Camp was like a live organism, growing, shrinking, and changing shape, depending on the people inhabiting it. As always, it thrummed with purpose. The snowpack felt firm under the women's snowshoes as they carried their loads into the encampment. They piled everything onto an unclaimed spot. Next to them was a line of matching tents stamped with the name of a popular guiding service.

Norma Jean led her teammates to the camp manager's tent to introduce them and pick up the fuel they had paid for in Talkeetna.

"You're in luck," the manager said. "The lower-mountain forecast is clear and calm for the next four to five days."

They set up camp in their short sleeves, while friends streamed by to say hi to Norma Jean. Some also knew Cindy from her climbs in the Chugach and Talkeetna ranges. The visits continued into dinner, while the women ate their first and last fresh vegetables of the expedition. The oranges they passed around for dessert would reappear in their dreams in the nights to come.

They snowshoed up the Kahiltna Glacier and then progressed expedition-style. Her teammates' awe stirred up memories. She recalled being on the mountain for the first time and seeing it through fresh eyes.

With Lynn's experience as a rafting guide and Norma Jean's Denali expertise, they fell into the role of co-leaders.

At 11 Camp, they caught up with the guided group from Base Camp. Norma Jean wished they were on the same schedule. It would give her confidence knowing she could observe the leaders and sense-check her decisions against theirs. She and her team buried a cache and reluctantly returned to 7,800 feet for the night.

They met the men again the next day at 11 Camp—packed and ready to take on Motorcycle Hill and Windy Corner.

"We probed this place when we got here," the guide told Norma Jean. "Didn't find any crevasses."

That was a relief, and, happily, the sites were move-in ready. The block walls hadn't been eroded by the wind, and the snow wasn't riddled with pee holes and tobacco splatter.

Mild weather hung with them as they spent three days acclimating at 11 Camp. It continued as they trudged up Motorcycle Hill and up and over the knuckles of Squirrel Hill on their way to drop gear at 14 Camp. Windy Corner remained uncharacteristically calm, and their main challenge was keeping their sleds behind them along the diagonal slope. Norma Jean could have rattled off a dozen stories about people and gear getting blown off this exposed bend in the trail. The crevasses just beyond it were infamous people-swallowers, and the team took extra care to step only in the boot prints of other climbers.

Compared to the narrow site they had left behind, 14 Camp was expansive. Tents were clustered in the center of the plateau. The guided group had lined out some extra space, and the women set up next to them. No one was more elated than Norma Jean.

Slightly apart from the climbing community stood a pair of brown, WeatherPort shelters used by Dr. Peter Hackett and his colleagues—the medical professionals of Medical Camp. Hackett, an elite climber and expert on high-altitude physiology and medicine, had established this outpost at 14 Camp several years earlier. His group conducted studies, assisted climbers who were ill and injured, and helped arrange evacuations off the mountain. They also shared their communications equipment and facilities with climbing rangers from the National Park Service.

Just days earlier, Hackett had taken part in a record-breaking, high-altitude helicopter rescue on nearby Cassin Ridge, a route up Denali that was east of the West Buttress.

Lynn, Katherine, and Cindy were fascinated by Hackett's operation. After promising Norma Jean they wouldn't become guinea pigs, they visited the WeatherPorts and watched the researchers at work. They noticed a tail wind as they snowshoed back to their own tents. Then a gust blasted through 14 Camp, forcing all the tents to shimmy in unison and warning them that Denali's patience had run out.

## CHAPTER 11
# A Triumph of Group Dynamics

Waiting out a storm with friends felt far better than toughing it out alone. The women worked in pairs to clear off the tents, shovel out the troughs in between them, and reinforce the walls. They swapped books and told stories. They plucked cookie crumbles from their emergency stash and tossed them into each other's open mouths.

"Dang," Katherine said, chewing. "I feel like I'm at a slumber party!"

"Right!" said Cindy. "With a whole bunch of cute boys next door."

"I never went to a slumber party that lasted—what?—three days so far?" Lynn said.

Norma Jean nodded.

"We're acclimated now. As soon as the storm breaks, we can get out of here and move up."

The skies grew calm the next day. After letting the snow settle for a few hours, the guided group of "cute boys" went first. Content to let them break trail, the Rascals spent extra time organizing their gear. They buried their sleds, which would be impossible to use on the upper mountain, and marked them with wands.

Headwall, the steepest part of the West Buttress route, lay ahead. It rose from about 14,300 feet to a col at 16,200 feet and bore fixed lines for climbers to clip into. Norma Jean couldn't help remembering the fight between Erica—the Women on Denali Expedition leader—and her boyfriend here eight years earlier. The memory always popped up as Norma Jean reached Headwall:

Erica hurling a coil of heavy rope at Jim. Jim catching it without losing his balance. Jim descending in a huff.

Today, the women's stored-up energy fueled a faster-than-normal climb up the face. They unclipped from the fixed lines at the top and made it to the ridge, where the guided group had stopped for a rest. The men were discussing the two Chinese climbers that Dan, the pilot, had talked about. They speculated about where exactly they had slipped, one after the other, before sliding into a crevasse.

Norma Jean hoped the talk wouldn't spook her friends. No one liked hearing gossip about other climbers' bad choices or bad luck, especially while standing at the same place it happened.

The exposed ridge received frequent beatings from the wind, and the Chinese climbers weren't the only ones to suffer its wrath. Each season, some hapless team got suckered in by the 360-degree views and set up camp here, only to have their entire outfit scooped up and scattered across the crevasse field. Today's mellow air was a blessing.

Aching quads and steep drop-offs forced the teams into a state of slow motion and intense concentration—a painful sort of meditation. The trail followed the ridgeline, widening and narrowing around rock pillars and often dipping down to the left. Two thousand feet below on that northern side was the Peters Glacier. On the right they looked back down Headwall to the large basin they'd left behind at 14,000 feet. Finally, an extra-steep section of trail topped them out at a plateau and took them around a bend to High Camp.

Even filtered through the clouds, the light was stark. Only the tips of most tents were visible above tall, double-thick snow walls. The hard snow didn't give underfoot. It took an hour to gouge out a hole deep enough to stockpile their supplies. With great care, the women picked their way back down the ridge and descended Headwall to spend a final night in 14 Camp.

The next day's climb up Headwall and along the blustery ridge proved harder. Wind and fatigue tore at their resolve. At High Camp, Norma Jean steeled herself for the work ahead. It was best to stay in motion. After a handful of granola and a few gulps of water, they began digging their tent platforms and quarrying blocks of snow.

Later, the inside of the tent beckoned with the promise of rest. Cindy was already buried in her sleeping bag, unmoving. Norma Jean pulled her hat over her eyes and ears and burrowed all the way into her own bag. Sleep didn't always come easily at elevation. A low-level anxiety accompanied each breath of thin air. But she'd done it before, and she knew her body would soon acclimate.

The team had eaten cold snacks for dinner, and her stomach felt tolerably full. Outside the tents, other climbers stayed quiet as they reserved energy for the final push to the summit.

She drifted off, but it was short lived. Her ears hurt. Something vibrated.

She sat up to listen. The noise and the air disturbance were intense.

Cindy sat up and poked her head from her sleeping bag.

"What is that?" she asked.

"It's a helicopter," Norma Jean said. "A big one."

They scrambled from the tent. Lynn and Katherine were already outside, as were most others in camp. Everyone was facing east, where a Chinook helicopter hovered over the Cassin Ridge. Its double rotors chopped the air with great force. Two other Chinooks circled in the distance.

"Isn't that the same ridge they plucked someone off last week?" Katherine asked.

Lynn nodded. "The highest heli rescue ever."

An Army medic dangled from the hovering craft. He rode the cable down to the ridge. His movements were blocked from their view, but a short time later, a lone climber was hoisted up to the helicopter.

"Unreal!" someone said.

Norma Jean shivered, yearning for her sleeping bag but unable to look away. The cable descended again, and a second climber was lifted to safety. Shortly thereafter, the medic rode up. The Chinooks flew away, and camp grew quiet. Climbers stood in clumps, comparing what they saw and what they knew. Everyone had heard about the rescue a week earlier. How bizarre that it had happened again at the same site.

Cindy shook her head.

"All these airlifts freak me out," she said. "They're not good omens."

Norma Jean wanted to reassure her, to remind her that there was really no such thing as an omen. Preparation, attention, common sense, and mutual care were real.

She settled on something simpler.

"We're making good choices," she said. "And we will continue to make good choices until we are back in Talkeetna, at the Fairview, placing our enormous drink orders."

Cindy smiled and disappeared into her sleeping bag again.

They woke hours later with the tent in their faces.

"Ack!" Norma Jean said. "It snowed."

She batted at the ceiling and knocked some of the load off. But the nylon drooped back down on top of her again.

"We've got you," Lynn said from just outside. "We're almost finished cleaning off ours."

Their mittens made a rhythmic scraping noise on the slippery fabric. When the tent stood upright again, Norma Jean and Cindy climbed out to help re-dig the trenches around their little camp.

"I'm surprised the wind isn't worse," Cindy said.

She'd spoken too soon. Denali took a deep breath and exhaled.

Gale after gale swept in with sideways snow. The blizzard continued the rest of the day and into the night. The longer it shrieked, the higher it pushed Norma Jean's anxiety level. Her mind flashed back to a cramped, cold snow cave and the raw pains of hunger.

Forty-eight hours later, the wind and snow abated and the clouds receded higher into the sky. The friendly climbers and guides started consolidating their camp. The Rascals gathered in Norma Jean and Cindy's tent.

"Well," Norma Jean said, "what do you guys think? Should we make a run for the summit?"

They exchanged looks and Katherine broke out in a grin.

"You bet!"

"Yes!"

"Let's do it!"

Norma Jean held out her hand and they all slapped her five.

They wore their heaviest clothes but packed lightly. If Denali cooperated, they were in for a 12-hour round trip to the summit. They brought enough food for two cold meals and snacks and water in insulated bottles, along with their sleeping bags and pads and waterproof covers. Norma Jean also carried a stove, fuel bottle, and pot for additional water. They weighted down their tents with unused gear and collapsed them.

The men and their guides finished packing. Norma Jean felt thankful they were again willing to break trail. The men moved swiftly up the Autobahn, and the Rascals lagged behind. Katherine, who led, stopped every few steps. She looked upslope and then down, and Norma Jean wondered what was going on in her head. Was she remembering Norma Jean's story about nearly sliding to her death here? The recollection made her shudder, but she forced herself into the present. Better to focus on where she was placing her feet.

By the time they reached Denali Pass, their pace had slowed to one step for every two to three breaths. They walked slightly faster at the Football Field. Norma Jean was overjoyed there were no plumes blowing off the summit ridge. The group rested and ate before Pig Hill, and then Norma Jean took over as lead. About halfway up, she realized she was past the place she had been knocked to her knees two years before. This was uncharted territory for her. How rewarding to take it on with Lynn, Cindy, and Katherine.

Puffy cornices bulged along the summit ridge. Both sides of the quarter-mile-long, knife-edge trail dropped off thousands of feet. Clouds socked them in, walling off the view. The four women clipped into the running protection set by the group ahead of them. The trail offered no room for a thoughtless step as it led up and down the spiky, snow-covered contours of the ridge. The sounds of heavy breathing mingled with the light wind.

Half an hour later, they arrived at the south summit, the highest point in North America. The sky rolled out gray and flat, underpinned by clouds. The women stooped, resting hands on thighs, as they labored to get enough air. A flicker of pride overcame Norma Jean's exhaustion.

Lynn tromped over. Tears soaked into the scarf covering her lower face. She threw her arms around Norma Jean and danced her side to side. "You did it! You made it! You summited Denali!"

"I did," she said. "We did."

Katherine and Cindy joined in. It felt cozy inside their circle. The whole experience was so much warmer, so much richer than her solo attempt two years before. Why, she wondered, had she ever wanted to go it alone?

## CHAPTER 12
# Culture Clash

**May 1989**

Alone was how she felt, though, the following year, when she had her first chance to be the lead guide for Genet Expeditions on Denali. Alone and awkward.

It was May 1989. Norma Jean, her boss Harry, and their newly arrived Japanese client, Kiyoshi, sat together in the pulsing lights of a strip club—or a "gentlemen's club," as Harry put it. He had thought the place would put the 40-year-old climber at ease after his long flight, but the gesture was one of a few key misunderstandings.

Kiyoshi scowled through the gyrating performances and winced each time a piece of lingerie dropped to the floor. He never looked higher than a dancer's feet. He drank only water and firmly shook his head when Harry offered him something stronger.

The next morning, when they picked him up for the drive to Talkeetna, Kiyoshi remained aloof. His expression hadn't changed much overnight, except now his knitted brows were accentuated by bags under his eyes. His face telegraphed disapproval and disgust more clearly than any words could: He did not want a woman guiding him on the mountain. As they walked along Main Street, he kept his head bowed as though deeply ashamed.

Norma Jean taught Kiyoshi how to rescue himself from a crevasse. Inside an empty warehouse, they slung their ropes over a beam and suspended themselves in the air to simulate a fall. She showed him how to fashion Prusik loops that would slide up his rope and serve as a place to step higher and higher. They also went over how he should anchor himself if Norma Jean, his rope partner, fell in. Kiyoshi studied her movements and mastered the skills within half a day. Unless she was demonstrating something, he did not look at her directly.

At Base Camp, they met a bilingual Japanese climber who offered to translate. Norma Jean then gave Kiyoshi the spiel she would have normally provided before they left Talkeetna. He nodded, occasionally interjecting with commentary the translator did not share with her. Instead, the bilingual man would shake his head and look at his feet.

It felt grim setting off into such a massive wilderness with someone who disdained her. Safe climbing depended on mutual trust. Kiyoshi obeyed her cobbled-together instructions, but he remained stiff and avoidant during their stopovers. He ate so little that she routinely gave his leftovers to other teams, and, despite her urgings, he didn't seem to drink enough water. He refused to use the pit latrines she had dug, making it impossible to monitor the color of his urine and determine whether he was staying hydrated. It appeared he wasn't peeing or pooping at all. Reaching the summit would be impossible if he made himself sick or ran out of energy; surely he knew this. Yet he couldn't bring himself to void into the same pit as her?

A brief storm chased them down to 11 Camp, and another held them at 14 Camp, but overall they made steady progress. She began to feel hopeful. At High Camp, battered climbers stumbled in from the summit, with a windstorm on their heels. Norma Jean and Kiyoshi waited for it to pass, until a weather window opened up ... a small one.

They would go for it.

Norma Jean had a feeling of foreboding as they ascended the Autobahn. Experience had taught her how short and unpredictable breaks in a storm could be. To make it up and back, she and Kiyoshi had to climb swiftly, with as few breaks as possible. She had tried to communicate this to him, but all he seemed to grasp was that they were heading up. For the first time in two weeks, he looked her in the face and smiled.

They crested the Autobahn and plodded up to Denali Pass. As if in slow motion, Kiyoshi lumbered over to an exposed rock face and leaned against it for a rest. His cheeks were flushed and his breaths came in heavy puffs. The wind picked up.

A team caught up and trudged past them. The leader grunted hello, while the others waved clumsily. They knew, as she did, the clear skies would not last long. On their upward march, the group split into two, like a river flowing around a boulder. Another team behind them repeated the formation, breaking into two lines and snaking around some mysterious obstacle.

Norma Jean peered after the second group to see what it was. She blinked to clear her vision, and the obstacle moved. It was a climber. No, two climbers. Staggering down toward them. Falling, getting up. Trying again.

It would be good to get a closer look. She tapped Kiyoshi.

"Ready?"

He held up a mitten and shook his head. Another ten minutes passed before he would move.

The struggling climbers had stopped completely by the time they reached them.

"Can you help us?" asked the closer one. His words were slurred and "help" came out as "hep." His balaclava was cockeyed, allowing one frosty eyebrow to poke out.

Kiyoshi ignored them, but Norma Jean could not.

She took a breath, stalling for a few seconds as she reassured herself. Her answer would change everything. For the two climbers. For her client. For her career.

"Yes," she said, "of course."

She called out to Kiyoshi. He stopped and continued facing upslope while she questioned the pair. Steve and Doug, guys in their thirties, first time on Denali, had rushed to the summit but gotten caught in the storm that had stalled Norma Jean and Kiyoshi at High Camp. The men said they had frostbitten their hands and feet. They were likely hypothermic.

Nothing could be done for Steve and Doug in the growing roar of Denali Pass. Taking off their gloves to examine their hands could worsen their frostbite. Staying still would make them colder: The best remedy for hypothermia was movement.

"We're going to escort you down to High Camp," she said. "But hold on. I have to talk to my client."

She hiked up to Kiyoshi and stood in front of him. She dipped her head toward the climbers.

"They are sick. We will help them get down."

His ski mask and goggles couldn't disguise the rigidity of his face. Undoubtedly, he thought they had a chance to beat the coming storm. Undoubtedly, he thought she was wrong for choosing to assist the injured climbers rather than leading him to the summit.

She strode down to Steve and Doug. Kiyoshi hesitated for several seconds, then followed.

Norma Jean bent down to adjust Doug's balaclava. She tightened the straps on his backpack and helped him onto his butt so she could check his crampons. Sure enough, they were on loose and crooked, and one had gotten snagged inside a pantleg. She freed it and snugged the crampons against his boot soles.

Pulling Steve's hat down over his ears, she rezipped his parka up over his chin. His lips were cracked, the corners caked with dried spit. She handed him her water bottle, and he drained it.

She hooked Steve on to her rope and Doug to Kiyoshi's, tugging the hardware and testing the knots to confirm everything was secure. The men's frostbitten fingers were useless for any fine-motor tasks, and they wobbled on their numb, damaged feet. She hoped Kiyoshi, despite his qualms, would cooperate with her to get the pair to safety.

"I'll lead," she said, putting her hand on her chest.

She pointed at each of them.

"Then Steve. Doug, you're first on your rope, and Kiyoshi is last."

Norma Jean found Kiyoshi's ice axe, placed it in his hand, and tried to look him in the eye. He averted his gaze, but nodded to show he understood: If Doug fell in Denali Pass or on the Autobahn, Kiyoshi would have to sink the axe into the snow to arrest their fall. Realistically, they might both slide to their deaths, but it was the only hope.

They positioned themselves and with slow, careworn steps, started down.

Norma Jean had no idea how many hours passed before they reached High Camp. Constant vigilance combined with the physical labor of shuttling back and forth to check on Steve and Doug had sacked her.

"Where is your campsite?" she asked, straining to get the words out.

Steve stared, while Doug looked around wildly.

"I think. I think, maybe, uh, it's that way?"

He slung his arm in a random direction.

Norma Jean breathed a few times. Searching for their site would be a waste of precious energy. At least the men had their sleeping bags in their summit packs.

She put up her tent, installed the pair inside, and reinforced the snow walls. Kiyoshi erected his own tent and disappeared inside. He was capable of taking care of himself.

The wind was building, and clouds fogged the other peaks. She stumbled through camp in search of a climbing ranger or others with medical experience, but no one among the half dozen tent sites could help her. Most people were battered and dazed from their own clashes with the mountain.

The exertion from the downclimb had warmed Steve and Doug, and Norma Jean quit worrying about hypothermia; frostbite was another matter. Back inside the tent, she removed their mittens and wrapped their hands in bandages.

Their feet fared worse. Each step had borne the excruciating weight of their bodies. Gravity had jammed their blistery toes into the nose of their boots. Norma Jean removed their socks one by one to find a purplish, oozing mess. She cleaned the feet and toes and also bandaged them.

The next hours were a constant routine of melting snow in the pot on her stove and getting as much liquid down the pair as possible. Water, cocoa, tea, soup—all of it would help keep the frostbite from deepening. Aspirin reduced swelling and provided the slightest relief from the agony of thawing fingers and toes. From here down, it would be vital to keep the men's extremities from refreezing.

The all-night twilight allowed her to keep an eye on Steve and Doug inside the tent. She peered at them every hour or so and listened for ragged breathing or other issues; their slumber was steady and deep. She checked in on Kiyoshi in his tent. He, too, slept quietly.

• • •

The doctors at Medical Camp were busy attending to others, so Norma Jean re-dressed Steve and Doug's hands and feet, herself. Swelling made it nearly impossible to get one of Steve's boots back on, and Kiyoshi had to help. As he twisted and shoved the foot back in, Steve howled and Kiyoshi looked at him worriedly.

"Gomen'nasai," he said meekly. "Sorry."

So he did have some compassion. A faint hope hovered in the back of her mind. Perhaps he could forgive her now that he'd had to reckon with the men's injuries.

"Your swelling concerns me," she said to Steve and Doug. "We need to go all the way to Base Camp and get you on a flight out. Can you do that?"

Both looked panicky but agreed to try.

Norma Jean and Kiyoshi picked up their cached food, fuel, snowshoes, and sleds at 13,500 feet. A trio of good Samaritans led Steve and Doug around the worst of Windy Corner while Norma Jean and Kiyoshi wrestled with their own sleds.

Other teams helped them manage icefalls and hidden crevasses around and below 11,000 feet. But when they reached the final stretch on the Kahiltna, everyone waved goodbye as they snowshoed or skied on ahead. The lure of Base Camp and its waiting bush planes was too great.

Norma Jean led her team along the glacier, while Kiyoshi brought up the rear. Having lost their snowshoes, Steve and

Doug wore their climbing boots and crampons, which put them at greater risk for punching through crevasses. Norma Jean took slow, deliberate steps and stayed mindful.

The men whimpered with each footfall up Heartbreak Hill. Norma Jean shuddered, imagining the pain in their tattered feet and swollen hands. By the time they reached Base Camp, the camp manager had secured places for them on the next flight out.

• • •

"Kiyoshi complained," Harry said as they sat in his office two days later.

Norma Jean nodded. This was not news.

"Tell me about the trip," he said. "From your perspective."

It took a good twenty minutes to relay the story and most of its relevant details. She tried to be dispassionate, to scrub her voice of the frustration she felt toward Kiyoshi and the sympathy for Steve and Doug.

"And what happened when you landed back in Talkeetna?"

"I'd gotten hold of my mom. She met the plane, and we rushed Steve and Doug to Providence in Anchorage. They're still being treated."

Harry cocked his head, a bemused look on his face.

"Well, first I got Kiyoshi a cab and helped him load up his pack and gear."

"Ah," he said, smiling but pursing his lips. "Kiyoshi. Our client."

Norma Jean blushed.

Harry leaned back in his chair and looked up at the ceiling. He was good at letting silence do the talking. Although he was only four years her senior, he seemed wiser, more adult. He had been her boss on and off since she was a teenage counselor at his wilderness camp.

"You are a kind person with a tender heart, but no one else on that mountain was your responsibility."

Norma Jean willed her face to cool down.

"But they begged me. They couldn't walk. They were slurring their words. People were swinging wide around them like they were lepers."

Then, trying to fill the space, she added something regrettable.

"Besides," she continued, "there was only a small break in that storm. I'm not sure Kiyoshi and I could have gotten up and back in time."

"Not sure?" he said.

"That's right. He wasn't moving very fast."

"Nonetheless, you should have shown him that you were giving it everything you had. He should have felt confident that he was your priority. That didn't happen."

She opened her eyes wide and rapid-blinked to restrain the tears.

"I realize he wasn't an easy or cooperative client. Perhaps not the best match. But you wanted to prove yourself as a lead guide, and he was the one in the queue. Sometimes that's just the way it goes."

This was it, then. She had blown her first and only chance at being a lead guide, something she'd worked toward her whole career. Nothing else that Harry said registered. She left his office dazed.

Tears spilled down her cheeks as she drove away from Genet Expeditions. Where to go? Not home. She wasn't ready to utter the words out loud. Or to share the bad news with her new husband, Clark. Without thinking, she found herself heading to the Lazy Mountain trailhead. A long, lung-busting run would help her get through this. Bleed off the adrenaline and feed the body's post-expedition craving for more suffering.

The sharp grade forced all thoughts aside as her body shifted into mountain mode. Her breathing was heavy, but her legs felt powerful, so accustomed were they to propelling her up the steeps. She lunged up-trail through cottonwood and birch that grew sparser and then shrank to mere saplings before petering out completely. She sprinted along the summit ridge and climbed over two rock outcroppings before reaching the last and tallest.

Lazy Mountain's top overlooked the tangled strands of the Knik River and the farmlands outside of Palmer. Snow-streaked mountains encircled it. Denali stood some 120 miles off to the north, though high clouds blocked the view today. She closed her eyes and pictured it, relived a few of the challenges she'd faced with Kiyoshi, Steve, and Doug.

She wondered how she would look back on the Denali trip ten or 20 years from now. Would she feel glad she had helped? Happy for the men who lived through hypothermia and got to keep their fingers and toes? Or sad that she hadn't gone all out to get her client to the summit?

She'd done the ethical thing, made her choice out of conscience, and time would prove her right. She knew this, yet she still felt defeated. She had to push back somehow. Take action. If not, her feelings might fester and swell and crowd out her proud legacy of mountaineering.

There was one way she could think of to redeem herself. It would be the ultimate counter-punch against this unbearable self-doubt. The piece of business she'd left unfinished in '86. She would return to Denali and attempt another solo summit.

CHAPTER 13

# Team of One—The Sequel

**May 1990**

A year later, the evening of May 29, 1990, 31-year-old Norma Jean Saunders and pilot Jim Okonek landed on the Kahiltna. The plane glided along like a boat, rising and dipping over tiny swells on the glacier's surface as it came to a stop. They deplaned, and Jim unloaded Norma Jean's gear.

"This is why I don't worry about you going alone," he said, pointing to the pile. "It's obvious you know what you're doing. You've got your gear down to just the essentials."

He pulled out a ten-foot, aluminum ladder and set it down next to her sled. The ladder was painted red and decorated with black ravens. It would replace Bridgit, the crevasse-rescue contraption she had worn in 1986.

"Fancy," Jim said, setting the ladder in the snow. "The one Vern used a couple of years back was just plain, unpainted aluminum."

She nodded and smiled.

In 1988, Vern Tejas had made a solo summit of Denali in the winter. He was the first climber to do so and return safely. Vern and Norma Jean were old friends and longtime coworkers at Genet. She had sought his advice several times about her solo.

In addition to the ladder, a few things had changed in the way Norma Jean approached her Denali attempt this time around. She had learned that in order for her solo to be considered legitimate, she had to do everything from scratch. No clipping into anyone else's lines. No food or drinks prepared by other hands. No moving into abandoned campsites. Maybe it was lucky she hadn't made it to the summit four years earlier. Someone surely would have challenged her on it.

For this trip, she would pace herself based on how she felt, climbing alpine style instead of expedition style. The newer, faster method meant carrying gear as high as she safely could in a single day and sleeping there for only as many nights as it took to acclimate. No more ascending Denali like an inchworm.

She napped in Base Camp and woke late at night to break down camp and make her way over to Heartbreak Hill. How would she feel next time she was here, skiing up it? Hopefully, less like last year with Kiyoshi, Steve, and Doug and more like two years ago, with Lynn, Cindy, and Katherine.

She wore the ladder in the same position she'd worn Bridgit, with her body harnessed in the center and the frame jutting out in front and behind. The sled was attached at the back, and the ladder kept it from nipping at her heels as she skied down-hill. Her pack and sled were at their heaviest, with the load split about fifty-fifty, but the kit fit her well. She felt confident.

The sky was royal blue, a shade so pure it looked almost unnatural. No clouds drifted in to diffuse the sunshine, and soon she was sweating. Halfway across the Lower Kahiltna, she stopped to chug water and strip down to her jog bra.

Norma Jean assembled a hearty lunch at the 7,800-foot camp—a mangled sandwich that she'd forgotten to eat in Base Camp, a cup of soup, a baggie of granola, and a brownie. The food picked up where her adrenaline had tapered off, and she skied and skinned up almost another 3,000 vertical feet after lunch. She overnighted at 10,500 feet, a flat area just shy of 11 Camp. Other climbers had left caches here and continued on to the more established site to sleep, so she was alone. She turned in early, hunkering down in her bag and surrendering to her dreams.

In one, she lifted off from Bird Ridge in her paraglider. Clark floated above her, calling out, laughing, and cawing like a raven. As the wind hoisted them, the slope fell away and the gray, churning waters of Turnagain Arm raged below. The scene was a rerun of dozens of flights they had taken around the Chugach as part of her Denali training last summer. They had spent the winter in Utah hiking, running, skiing, and paragliding at higher altitudes in the Wasatch and Uinta Mountains.

Clark, an experienced climber and Genet veteran, had acted as a sounding board during Norma Jean's preparations and helped with organizing gear and apportioning food. He had fashioned the attachment that connected her harness to her ladder. In honor of their small guiding company, Raven Adventures, he had drawn their black, raven-head logo on every last bit of equipment.

She opened her eyes at 6 a.m. to find the logo beaming up at her from her sleeping pad.

"Get up!" it seemed to say. "Time to explore the sky."

Soon she skinned her way up to 11 Camp, chatted with a guide she knew there, and moved on. She was strong, almost unbelievably so. All systems worked in concert: muscles making her load feel light, heartbeats in check, breathing hard but manageable. Her body was sending an uninterrupted signal to her brain: "Go-go-go-go-go!"

Blowing snow at Windy Corner shrouded the crevasses. She checked the connection points between her harness and ladder more than once. The cracks were worst at the apex, where the glacier fractures as it moves around the bend. Here, she made halting, serpentine progress. Beyond, the route grew slightly less hazardous. She cached her lower-mountain gear and her ladder, skis and sled. Suddenly, she felt nimbler. She felt high.

Then her foot pierced the snow. She dropped a meter, one leg sticking straight down into the crevasse, the other bent up against her chest. The snow that had fallen in with her began crumbling and dropping away. She grabbed her ice axe and levered herself up, bit by bit, until she was out. She crawled away from the opening before rising, shakily, to her feet. The hole she left behind was tiny and hard to see.

She continued on with extreme care, probing with a ski pole and testing her weight before each footstep. Slow and cautious. Her breath quavered, and anxiety filled her stomach like a bag of sand. Fourteen Camp, which had recently seemed so close, felt miles off. Too many steps, too many hazards, too many hellish crevasses between here and there, when all she wanted was to curl up in her tent and forget.

"I promise," she bargained, "if I get there, I will ignore the urge to just keep going. I will stop and rest so I can focus better from here out. I won't make another mistake like this one."

At 14 Camp, she built one of her best sites yet, digging down an extra foot and crafting the highest wind walls she could manage. She checked her tent stakes and repositioned the tie-outs. Dinner was a double serving of Mountain House spaghetti and a bonus brownie. She allowed herself to sleep a full twelve hours. In the morning, she melted snow for a sponge bath and hair wash. She inventoried her food and reorganized her pack so the most indispensable gear was at her fingertips. She made cups of tea for herself and visited with friends. At 9:00, she turned in, happily anticipating another night of motionless sleep.

In drowsy moments, she reminisced about her family's dogs romping around the yard or hiking by her side. She could almost hear the tags jingling from their collars. Rascal was a small, white Sealyham terrier, cuddly but with loads of energy. He was prone to sitting on his hind legs like a prairie dog. Harpo, a Dalmatian her parents acquired later, accompanied her on hikes and runs as she trained for Denali. Such happy memories. Slowly, though, she realized that the pleasant chiming sound wasn't just her imagination. She opened her eyes; the tent's zipper pulls were clinking together. The wind was growing.

It was impossible to know how long it had been happening. She dressed and crawled out into the open. Five inches of snow covered her tent. She circled around, brushing it off, and heading back inside to retrieve her avalanche shovel. Clearing the site would buy her another 90-minutes' rest before she had to do it again.

Soon the wind rose up and pelted 14 Camp with snow. Gusts rolled in like earthquakes. She hunkered down in her sleeping bag and covered her ears. Once, after sleeping longer than intended, she sat up to find the walls pressing inward. The tent's apex was barely wide enough for her head. She scrambled out of her bag and into her coat. But the tent zipper was frozen shut.

"Seriously."

She leaned in close and exhaled onto the track on either side of the zipper pulls. Her hot breath melted the frost between the zipper's interlocking teeth. She continued, millimeters at a time, blowing and tugging, blowing and tugging, until the entire track had released. When she at last opened the fly, a foot of snow toppled in over her knees.

The other teams took turns clearing their campsites, so Norma Jean glimpsed different people each time she ventured outside. Performing all the camp duties by herself taxed her, and loneliness made it worse. If the snow piled up on her nonporous, waterproof tent, would she suffocate in her sleep? If the storm lasted longer than a week, would she run out of food before she could summit? She missed Clark. She missed Lynn, Katherine, and Cindy: such a selfless group, with each woman insistent on doing more than her share. They had teased one another about being aggressively considerate.

She did have the occasional visitor. Her guide friends Dave Staeheli and Nick Parker tromped over to check on her, as did their assistants. She felt grateful for the company—and for the breaks in the monotony, fear, and frustration of a seemingly endless storm.

She emerged on the sixth morning to a cobalt sky. The edges of the campsites were softened under three feet of new snow, and the Alaska Range glimmered in the distance. Though Denali's summit was clear, no one had started up Headwall toward 16 Ridge.

The other tents were quiet. Norma Jean wandered around and listened for signs of fellow early risers, but all she heard was the occasional sound of snoring. This was understandable, as it was much easier to sleep without the wind's racket, yet also kind of hard to understand, since Mother Nature had cleared the way for them to continue up the mountain.

She made a triple serving of oatmeal and added crushed nuts and M & Ms.

Dave Staeheli plodded away from his camp on his way to the latrine. When he returned, Norma Jean greeted him.

"I bet your clients are clawing at the walls," she said.

He laughed. "You know it."

"When are you guys breaking camp?"

"Not right away," he said. "We want to dry out the tents and all the other soggy stuff."

"Really? On a day like this?"

"Really. Gotta preserve Genet's gear."

He turned and looked up Headwall. "It's safer to let the snow settle down, too."

She nodded. Avalanche danger compounded after each big snowfall. But, having stayed in camp days longer than expected, she was jonesing to get going again. The climb would be much less difficult with others breaking trail.

She asked Nick Parker, but he felt the same. So did every other team in camp.

"Guess I'm on my own," she said, packing up her wet tent and gear. Everything would quickly dry in the gales of High Camp.

Norma Jean buried a cache of two days' food and fuel near the medical shelters and marked it with red and black Raven Adventures wands. She said her farewells and waded through hip-deep powder toward Headwall.

## CHAPTER 14
# Heavy Load

"Am I insane?" Norma Jean wondered.

Climbers are a competitive species, and she had expected that when others saw that she was actually taking on Headwall, they would follow, maybe try to catch up and pass her. Yet halfway up, she remained alone. Why had every single climber in 14 Camp chosen this moment to respect the danger of avalanches?

The fixed lines were inches beneath the surface, but she knew better than to try to lift them out and attach a jumar. Not as a solo climber.

She toed away the powder before plunging her boot deep into the snowpack. Still, she had to nose around with her foot to find the underlayer and drive her crampons in. Each step took maximum effort and too much time. Her pack was heavy with food, upper mountain attire, and most of the gear from her sled. She lodged her ice axe in at shoulder level and took another vertical stride. With so much force against her, it felt like climbing a waterfall. A line from a Springsteen song circled her mind like a record with a skip.

"One step up and two steps back."

She leaned into the slope for a water break. Headwall was taking forever, and she would have to keep breaking trail, even when she reached 16 Ridge. The realization made her want to cry. She stifled it and tucked her water bottle back into her coat. Hours later, though, she noticed someone was mewling in time with her movements. A glance behind her revealed she was still alone.

"Sheesh," she said, shaking her head.

Then she did a double take. Far below, some climbers were starting up Headwall. She returned to her slog, trying to get as high as she could before they caught her. It was a matter of pride. As she neared the top and at last released the tears of exhaustion, the men caught and passed her.

"Thanks for breaking trail!" one called out.

"Look at you go!" said another.

"Good job! You're strong!"

She sat in the snow and chuckle-sobbed. Though it had arrived late, her wish had come true. The teams would plow a trail up the rocky spine of 16 Ridge and make her next few hours infinitely less difficult. She wiped her face and drank some water, determined to keep going.

Loose snow sluffed from the ridge and trickled down into the void on either side. She climbed here with her heart in her throat, as always. Eager to stay ahead of any venturis that might funnel through, she pushed away her tiredness to keep up a steady pace. She eased past the granite tower of Washburn's Thumb about halfway up and pressed on. Mercifully, there would be no ambushes by the wind today. She rounded the corner into High Camp.

Creating a campsite at elevation was a special kind of chore, especially from scratch. She found a flattish spot at the edge of the settlement and dumped her gear. She sat on her backpack and stared blankly at her surroundings and the other slow-moving bodies. Her ten-minute rest stretched to thirty. Then she shook off her malaise and refocused her eyes and looked around for a span of windswept snow that would give in to her saw. It would be her snow-block quarry.

Her spent muscles set the pace, and camp construction took twice as long as it should have. The elevation and cold, dry wind made heating water an extra-long, extra frustrating task. Twice she spaced out and let most of the water evaporate before she could add it to the pouch of dehydrated chili mac.

She scarfed down her dinner and turned in. Sleep came in fragments. Her Saturday morning was spent packing for the summit, until a couple of teams arrived back in camp with reports of wind. Disappointed, she retired to her tent with a cup of cocoa and someone's water-stained paperback. Having another day to acclimate wasn't bad. But she couldn't ignore the tension that every climber felt at High Camp: It was too hard on the body to stay more than about five days. A summit opportunity had to present itself before then.

Sunday, June 10, 1990, dawned with news of climbers in trouble on Denali's West Rib route. A Japanese team of seven had left one member, an ailing man named Ito, at Archdeacon's Tower, near where the West Rib and West Buttress routes converge. Ito suffered from a bad cough, shortness of breath, and difficulty walking. The others had summited but then gotten separated in a whiteout. Some were able to locate Ito again but were unable to save him. The fragmented team stumbled into High Camp, distraught, frostbitten, and out of food and water.

Rangers tended their wounds, and other climbers fed them from their own stores of jerky and dehydrated soup. Someone approached her. "We're lowering the survivors to Medical Camp," he said. "Can you join in?"

Helping was second nature to Norma Jean. After all, she had spent most of her professional life assisting other mountaineers. On this climb, though, she could not clip into anyone else's lines—even as part of a rescue. Her stomach tensed as she forced out the words.

"I'm sorry. I can't help you."

The ranger nodded. "Understood."

"I can make cocoa, though," she said. "And tea."

"Yeah," he said. "Do it."

She assembled her stove on a snow table she had carved out near the entrance to her tent. She piled chunks of snow into a small pot and added more as it melted. Hot drinks she could make in her sleep. Others came by to donate teabags and cocoa. She spent her day collecting empty cups and returning them full and steaming.

The sky was on her mind as she worked. A gray strip of fog blocked out the distant peaks to the south and west, indicating that a wall of weather was grinding its way toward the summit. It was fast becoming a now-or-never moment.

With the Japanese climbers safely lowered to Medical Camp, the exhausted rescuers disappeared into their tents. It was 9:30 p.m. Norma Jean estimated a day or less until the storm hit. Her summiting gear was ready to go, so she packed up and headed for the ranger tent to say goodbye to her friend Randy Waitman. He was scrubbing a bowl with snow, staring intently and likely thinking about the day's tragedy. Would he try and talk her out of leaving?

"Randy?"

He jerked his head, his expression startled. Seeing she was ready to go, he lumbered over.

"Summit time?" He smiled wanly.

She nodded.

He stepped close and hugged her as tightly as their down parkas would allow.

"You go up there, Norma Jean," he said, voice breaking. "And you make it back down. Alive."

His tears were contagious. She pulled away to keep from crying into his parka.

• • •

With each leaden step along the Autobahn, she pressed down thoughts of the dead climber. She focused on each footfall, ensuring her crampons punctured the rock-hard snow every time. Side-hilling meant that gravity was always tugging at her ankles.

A panorama of mountains and sky surrounded her, all softened in the light of evening, but the view hardly mattered. She could only face forward, taking one slow-motion step at a time and breathing quick, shallow breaths. Her brain was engulfed in a bubble of fatigue and dread. Everything was heavy up here: Her smaller summit pack felt weightier than the crammed-full one she'd started with at Base Camp.

The body was not immediately ahead, this much she could see. But somewhere up there crouched the frozen remains of poor Ito.

Norma Jean made it up to Denali Pass. Here the route traced the backside of a ridgeline. She stared out at the violet sky and white mountains, hoping to store the picture in her memory for later.

The snow solidified as the grade steepened. Gripping the head of her axe, she drove it in just above shoulder level and followed up with two quick toe-steps. As she repeated the sequence, she struggled to move fluidly. The air was half as dense as at sea level.

She topped out on a steep pitch, and there he was. She sucked in cold air, then coughed it out. Ito was crouched into a ball, just off the path, not 30 feet away. His parka stood out like a traffic light. Archdeacon's Tower shot into the sky behind him. The trail was windswept, and her crampons grated the ice. The squeaking noise felt awful and disrespectful. Her throat tightened from the horror of it.

Oh, how she wished he weren't here. If only he could be back at Base Camp with his team, all of them whole and uninjured, drinking champagne and awaiting their flight to Talkeetna. In this better world, she would not have to walk past him. She closed her eyes and stood still, desperate to catch her breath.

If this man could not survive Denali, then what made her think she could?

"Stop," she whispered to herself. "Redirect your thoughts."

She inhaled, exhaled. Counted her breaths.

What would Ito say if he had a voice? Would he express regret for trying to push through a storm? No doubt his team felt pressured by the time limits on their travel visas. She was free of such pressures. He would want her to make good decisions. Yes, that was it. He wanted her to summit and to return safely. He wanted her to have the one thing he no longer did, the single thing that mattered.

She resumed her trek, but now her steps sounded different. Accompanying the squeaking of crampons on ice was the climber's voice.

"Live," he seemed to whisper. "Live."

## CHAPTER 15
# Taking her Place at the Top

Ito's image stayed with her as she crossed the Football Field: A hunched, brightly clad body contrasting with the flat, white snow. Though she hadn't looked at him directly, her imagination had filled in the details. The closed eyes and a nose black with frostbite, and, worse, the hours upon hours of suffering he must have endured before dying.

His teammates had suffered, too, from frostbite and regret. The death would haunt them in the years to come. Norma Jean knew plenty of survivors who lived every day with guilt, deserved or not.

She reached the base of the summit dome, where in 1986, the wind had beaten her back. Lucky timing had kept her from a fate like Ito's. Being here alone now made her anxious, and, without her beloved Rascals surrounding her, the anxiety mounted. Alone on Denali was so much scarier than alone on Lazy Mountain or alone in the Don Sheldon Amphitheater. Ahead, the exposed summit ridge was so very high—higher than she had climbed in two years. Could her legs take it? Would she be able to place each footstep precisely where it needed to go?

The combination of fear, fatigue, and elevation made it impossible to hold off more tears. She sank down for a good, long cry and wondered if she should even bother to keep going. She took off her goggles and wiped her eyes. She gazed out on the Football Field. Some dots appeared against the snow. People.

Yes, two of them. Bit by bit, the dots grew, and the strangest thought crossed her mind.

"They can't see me like this!"

She got to her feet. Powered by what she later described as pure, unadulterated ego, Norma Jean tightened the straps on her pack and resumed her quest. The hairline path along the summit ridge required total concentration. No space to reflect on how vulnerable she was.

At least now there was someone behind her.

The ridge widened as she closed in on the top. A wand bobbed in the breeze—a friendly wave to let her know she had arrived. A summit marker stuck out of the snow like an oversized pushpin. It was official! She slumped down and felt her voice accompany her breaths from exertion. Exhaled steam frosted her eyelashes, framing her view in white. The view. This was her second summit but her first time actually seeing the Alaska Range from this vantage point, with hundreds of smaller peaks rolling out to the horizon.

She slipped out of her backpack and fished out her camera.

The moon sat low in a sky of scattered clouds, with the sun rising behind her. There must be some sort of symbolism in their joint appearance, but she was too tired to recall. What time was it, anyway? She pulled back her sleeve: 4:05 a.m., six and a half hours from when she'd left High Camp. Six and a half hours of all-out effort and swinging emotions. No wonder she felt numb. She forced herself to stand up and take pictures.

Denali cast a shadow on the Ruth Glacier, the place where her climbing adventures had begun. Between her expeditions there and her work as an instructor for Genet, she had spent almost a full year of days on the Ruth. The glacier was surprisingly hard to recognize from this perspective, though.

An orange and gray band of sky outlined the mountaintops at the horizon, a glinting of sun off clouds that indicated an oncoming storm. Norma Jean felt it in her stomach.

It took the climbers—a man and a woman—45 minutes to reach her. The man called out first.

"Hooray for you!" he said, stopping for a few gasping breaths. "First woman to solo!"

They lumbered over and hugged her.

"So ... exciting!" the woman breathed. "We're. Your. Witnesses."

"Thank you. That means so much."

Having witnesses would distinguish her from another woman who, eight years before, had claimed to be the first female to summit Denali alone. Her name made the records but her story was never backed up by other people or even photographs.

Norma Jean's more immediate concern was the descent. It was considered the most dangerous part of any climb, and the fear of it buzzed in the back of her mind. She winced at the thought of passing Ito again. She dreaded down-climbing Denali Pass, so icy this year it had been hard to get her crampons to bite. Then, of course, the Autobahn, whose slope she would forever remember with her whole body.

Beyond were crevasses and icefalls, perils she would now face with tired muscles and mind.

She traded observations with the pair for a few minutes and pointed at the horizon.

"I don't think we've got more than eight hours until the storm hits," she said. "And this climb isn't really over until we're down safely. So ..."

"Off you go!" said the woman, who had begun to catch her breath. "We'll be close behind."

Every step, she reminded herself, was the most important step. With this philosophy, she made it over the gnarliest features of the upper mountain. At High Camp, Randy Waitman greeted her with another bear hug and an expression of relief. She told him about passing Ito and warned him of the coming storm.

She crawled into her tent for a catnap and breakfast before dismantling her site and resuming her descent. If the storm caught her, she would be warmer and breathe more easily waiting it out at lower elevations. She could dig up her extra stores of food, too. Randy broadcast on the park service's CB radio that she was continuing down.

At 14 Camp, the rangers applauded her. The clapping sound echoed across the basin, and other climbers came out of their tents to join in. For the first time, the solo—her *successful* solo summit of Denali—felt real. She stopped for hugs and high-fives, and her old friend, Denali Climbing Ranger Scott Gill, insisted she call her parents on the radio.

She braced herself for an onslaught of questions.

"Mother!" she said. "Can you hear me okay?"

Nothing. She tried again.

"Hello? ... Mom? Dad?"

"I'm on the line," Jean said. "How are you, dear?"

"Never better. I made it to the summit!"

"Oh, honey, how wonderful."

"Can you believe it?"

"That's just super. We are so proud of you."

Considering how worried she had been, Mother seemed casual today.

"Anything you need to know?" Norma Jean said. "Anything you want to ask?"

"No, no, not that I can think of. I'm a little winded. We just got in from taking Harpo to the vet. And, oh! Your brother got a new job!"

Scott clapped a mitten over his mouth and turned away, shaking. All over the mountain and across the state, CB users on the same frequency were listening in on the call. She could practically hear their laughter.

A haze had drifted in while she talked, and she decided to continue down.

She stopped to pick up her food and fuel cache and later, the ones with her skis, ladder, and sled. Eleven Camp was still free of fog; she was managing to stay ahead of the storm's edge. This sharpened her resolve, and she acknowledged the hope that she might actually get all the way home tonight.

Head down, she skied the Kahiltna to Heartbreak Hill. Her long strides grew shorter with the flattening terrain. As she began skinning upward, she fell into a trancelike state in which each movement felt distinctive and worthy of remembering. Her mind was in "record" mode, taking in the snow-filled gullies and couloirs that ran down the surrounding peaks; registering the air's growing moisture; capturing the way her skins allowed her skis to slip back a touch before catching on the snow; logging the chirp sounds her poles made as she planted them.

She had experienced these sensations many times. Why did it all feel so important now? Was it possible this would be her last Denali climb? Hard to imagine. She was only 31, and the mountain had been the centerpiece of her life for over a decade.

More applause awaited at Base Camp, the loudest and most raucous yet. She felt like a rock star. The camp manager patted her shoulder and pointed toward the airstrip.

"Your Concorde awaits."

Norma Jean peered through her glacier glasses to see Jim Okonek standing next to his Cessna. Two others flanked him: One looked like her husband with his arms full of something and the other sported the fluffy, black beard of Vern Tejas. He wore a big parka and was probably in camp to guide a team up the mountain.

"Well, I'll be!"

She waved her ski poles in the air. Clark bobbed his head, and Jim and Vern waved back. The crowd's clapping and hooting accompanied her as she skied over to the Cessna.

Clark greeted her with champagne, flowers, and fresh strawberries. They exchanged a quick kiss. Norma Jean stepped out of her skis, unhooked herself from the ladder, took off her pack, and detached the sled. She stacked everything up for Jim to stow in the plane. Then she gave Clark a proper hug and bestowed one on Vern as well.

"Congratulations, Norma Jean," the pilot said as he trudged back and forth, whittling down the pile. "I knew you had this."

She caught and hugged him.

"I didn't expect you to get here before me," she told Jim. "And, heavens to Betsy, you brought Clark!"

"I was listening to the rangers' transmissions, so I knew you were absolutely hauling down the mountain. I kept Clark at the ready," he said.

It was unusual for a pilot to fly a passenger to Denali who wasn't climbing or sightseeing. Insurance companies frowned on it. Jim seemed to read her mind.

"It's only right that your biggest supporter should be here."

He took her rapidly wilting bouquet and placed it on a seat inside the airplane, while the trio of climbers clinked glasses and took swigs of champagne. They devoured the strawberries.

Vern hugged her again and said he had to get back to his clients. They agreed to catch up after he returned.

"That may be a while," he said. "Weather's coming."

Norma Jean and Clark squeezed into the cabin and took their seats. Jim did a walkaround inspection and hustled into the cockpit. They taxied past other pilots and climbers hurrying to load their planes and board them. Jim accelerated and they glided and jounced down the rutted surface until they reached takeoff speed. Norma Jean stared out the window at the familiar scene, and, for the last time, felt the skis leave the airstrip at Kahiltna Base Camp.

Turbulence rocked the plane as Jim made a rapid ascent and broke through the clouds. He beelined it for Talkeetna. They learned later that they were among the last to leave before a massive storm moved in and locked everyone in place for days.

## CHAPTER 16
# Change in Course

**June 1990**

Norma Jean and Clark unpacked in the basement of their home in Palmer. Her tent and sleeping bag were draped over a clothes line, with her down parka, pile jacket, and pile pants dangling from hangers on either side. Sleeping pads lay half uncurled on the floor, while boots, mittens, liners, hats, and other sweat-encrusted items aired out on a card table. Her sled and ladder leaned against the wall next to her skis. The washing machine chugged through its heavy-duty cycle in the corner, as the smell of laundry soap infused the swampy air.

Norma Jean picked up her climbing harness and her backpack, which was still half full.

"Let's organize the rest of the stuff upstairs."

The doorbell rang as she trotted up the steps. Though she had been home less than 24 hours, she had received a dozen visitors already: her parents, her brothers, the Rascals, and friends from Genet. She set her gear down in the living room while Clark answered the door.

Mother and Dad again, and this time they brought a late lunch.

"We know how busy you are with unpacking," Jean said, "and thought you might not make time to eat."

Norma Jean rolled her eyes and smiled at Clark. He smiled back and shrugged.

Jean hurried inside with Norman close behind. Rain dripped off their jackets as they hung them on the coat rack. In the kitchen, they set out plates and bowls and unwrapped homemade sandwiches. Jean went to the stove and poured a Tupperware container of soup into a pan for warming.

As they ate, Norman pressed his daughter for more details. Several questions had popped into his mind in the hour since they'd last seen each other. His interest in the climb was sincere, his curiosity genuine. He delighted in her stories. Mother, too. Though she kept her reactions muted, always hoping Norma Jean would tire of her adventures and settle down to have a family.

"Will you be staying in town for a while now?"

"No, Mother." She collected dishes and took them to the sink to avoid Jean's face.

"We've got jobs as kayaking guides," Clark said. "We leave for Kachemak Bay the day after tomorrow."

Jean paused before responding.

"Oh."

The phone rang, and Norma Jean picked it up in the living room. The caller was Anchorage Daily News sports editor Lew Freedman, and he wanted to interview her. Norma Jean's story would appear in the paper and be reprinted with a photo spread in Alaska Magazine, which had a large, international circulation.

They agreed on a time the next day. She floated back to the table and shared the news. Norman chuckled. He clapped Clark on the back.

"She's going to need a manager. Sounds like a good job for you."

• • •

Norma Jean and Clark packed the car for the five-hour drive from Palmer to Homer. After so many visitors the past few days, it felt strange that no one came to see them off. A few miles past Anchorage, they caught a glimpse of Turnagain Arm, the southern appendage of the Cook Inlet that surrounds Anchorage. It winked in the fading sunshine, doing a solid impression of a tranquil, inviting body of water.

The highway dropped down to two lanes before it passed Potter Marsh Bird Sanctuary. It bent east at Beluga Point, then followed a curvy path, hemmed in by the Chugach Mountains on the left and silty, brown Turnagain Arm on the right. The tide was in, and Norma Jean scanned the water for whales.

"See any?" Clark asked.

"No."

"Still pretty early."

The all-white belugas and their blue-gray young wouldn't show up until mid-July, as they chased salmon through the inlet to their spawning streams. But there would be plenty of beluga and other whales where they were headed.

They drove around the eastern edge of Turnagain Arm and followed the highway south onto the Kenai Peninsula. As they approached Turnagain Pass, Norma Jean's ears popped. Wind rocked the car and rain pelted the windshield. It felt strange not having to worry about the weather.

At the Tern Lake Junction, they continued onto the Sterling Highway. They skirted Kenai Lake, with its startling emerald water, and crossed over to the northwest side of the peninsula before making it to the end of the road at Homer.

A water taxi ferried them to China Poot Bay, an estuary on the south side of Kachemak Bay and home to the wilderness lodge where they would work for the rest of the summer. They were eager to start. Norma Jean's expedition was expensive and had kept her from earning a paycheck for weeks.

She felt lucky to guide in such a serene place. After most expeditions, she had become restless within days of returning home. Ringing phones, car engines, barking dogs, and the normal sounds of life in the Matanuska-Susitna Valley would begin to grate on her. She'd long for mountain views unmarred by strip malls and gas stations.

Though China Poot Bay offered mellower scenery from Denali, it was no less spectacular. The Kachemak Bay Wilderness Lodge stood near the water's edge, and here the ocean was clear and blue or green or silver, depending on the sky. A beach of stones out front grew wider and narrower with the tides. Nearby cabins for guests and staff perched on giant boulders that dropped to the ocean. Spruce grew everywhere, even in the cracks of the boulders.

Lodge guests had been informed that Norma Jean and Clark were mountain guides and paragliding instructors. On kayaking trips in the estuary and nearby coves and on hikes in Kachemak Bay State Park, the guests gushed with questions. Clark spent little time indulging them before turning the spotlight back around. His philosophy: The focus should remain on the client. Besides, he argued, being humble about your achievements was part of the mountaineering code.

Norma Jean held more of a "don't hide your light under a bushel" mindset. Clients listened raptly as she told of crossing a glacier with only her good judgment and a ladder to keep her out of crevasses, hunkering down alone while a blizzard raged outside her tent, climbing up steep, windswept passes so icy her crampons barely took hold. They asked endless questions: Wasn't she lonely up there? Wasn't she scared? Whatever possessed her to climb by herself? Was it worth it?

Then, in late June, Lew Freedman's Anchorage Daily News article came out, and a group of guests arrived having read it.

"You're *her*? You're the first woman to solo Denali?!"

"You're about to become famous."

"We can say we knew you when!"

Several days later, her mother mailed her a copy of the Daily News article along with another surprise—a certificate of recognition from the Alaska State Legislature for completing her solo climb up Denali. The page-long acknowledgment had been read into the state's congressional record just over two weeks after her return. She showed the document to the owners, who in turn, told the guests. This only intensified their interest.

Norma Jean happily continued answering questions and embraced the role of budding celebrity. The tension between her and Clark thickened.

Was she showing off or simply enjoying some hard-earned respect?

Was he holding her back or merely encouraging her to be humble?

As happens with many disagreements, this one spilled into other areas of their marriage. It was far from settled when they returned home.

Clark accepted a position at Alyeska Ski Area for the winter, and they moved from Palmer to Girdwood. As pioneers and VIPs in the world of Alaska paragliding, they were invited to a U.S. Hang Gliding Association meeting in San Francisco. The meeting's purpose was to set uniform standards for the teaching of paragliding, which was a newer and less established sport than its rigid-wing counterpart.

Clark had to report to work, so Norma Jean attended alone. While there, she was approached by one of the owners of Chandelle San Francisco Sky School. He wanted to expand the school's hang-gliding offerings to include paragliding instruction. Would she come to California to start up the new branch?

A difficult conversation with Clark awaited Norma Jean upon her return to Girdwood. The position would keep them apart for months at a time, and traveling back and forth for visits was too expensive. They talked it over, examined the implications, argued, and landed on opposite sides. She accepted the position.

Just before she left, Lew Freedman's 4,000-word feature story, "At Last, Alone at the Top," appeared in Alaska magazine. It included a variety of pictures of Norma Jean: skiing on the Kahiltna glacier; washing her hair outside her tent; and riding bikes with Clark in Hatcher Pass during her training. Another showed Clark on his knees at Denali's summit, radio in hand, proposing to Norma Jean, who was at Base Camp. The cover photo was a quirky, studio shot instead of one taken in the field. Wearing a colorful, brand-new climbing outfit, she dangled from a rope and smiled for the camera. She had requested that the cover photo be taken on Denali—or at least somewhere in the mountains—but the photographer had other plans.

Some in the mountaineering community ribbed her about the picture, complaining that it was staged. One longtime friend was particularly cutting, and his criticism stung. An Alaska magazine reader used the photo as an excuse to skewer the entire publication. He stated in a letter to the editor: "Never in my 55 years have I written to a magazine, but your November 1990 issue with the little cutie on the cover looks more like a Madison Avenue product than a product about the Alaska I know. I believe that you fill whole pages with fancy photos and a dozen or so words in an effort to add bulk to a publication that no longer contains any substance."

Although there were at least as many positive reactions to the story and its cover photo, the criticism stung. It felt like a good time to press "pause" on climbing. She had spent a huge chunk of her life navigating snow and ice, altitude and bitter cold wind. She'd met a succession of mountaineering goals dating back to her teen years, but being at the pinnacle didn't bring the satisfaction or clarity she had imagined. She wondered, what would it be like to leave it, veer away and immerse herself in the newer, faster-paced sport of paragliding.

CHAPTER 17
# Ready to Fly

**1990-1993**

"Ready to fly?"

A wide-eyed look of joy and fear spread across the face of Norma Jean's student, Chad, a 40-something special effects engineer from San Francisco. They stood on the second-lowest training hill. Connected to him by fifty-four taut suspension lines, his yellow canopy quivered on the grass behind him, puffed out and ready to rise.

"I am, indeed!" he answered.

"Okay, you know what to do," she said.

Chad bent at the waist, toggles in hand, and sprinted twenty yards to where the slope steepened. Norma Jean ran backward alongside him and yelled encouragement. He raised his arms into a Y.

The wind caught Chad's canopy and whisked him skyward.

"Hot diggity dog!" he yelled, voice trailing off as he rose.

She spun around to watch. She spoke into her radio, guiding his short flight. He demonstrated left and righthand turns, proving he had listened well during the days of classroom instruction and onsite demonstration. Assuming a safe arrival in the landing zone, he would progress to the next-higher slope. She couldn't wait to tell him.

In her three-year tenure with Chandelle, she had stopped counting the number of students she'd taught, although she remembered the faces and names and flights, the shared thrill of taking to the air, the gentle and not-so-gentle landings. The job allowed her to lean into her nurturing side, and her friendships blossomed.

Chandelle's training grounds stretched across a gentleman rancher's property near Point Reyes National Seashore, 80 minutes north of San Francisco. Thick sea air blew steadily and diffused the scent of wildflowers and mint across the rolling hills. Cows and sheep grazed in the distance.

People were often surprised to learn of Norma Jean's previous life as an Alaska mountaineer. Coastal California contrasted sharply with Denali, right down to the color palette and predictability of temperature and wind. Life at sea level was mellow and sweet.

Norma Jean and Clark had taught paragliding in Alaska during the summers, though they always kept their regular jobs. Here she was immersed, sometimes seven days a week, months at a time, in the sport. She took students on field trips to hone more advanced skills.

One such trip—a "soaring clinic" in which students would learn to enhance their ability to ride air thermals—took place on Marshall Peak, in the San Bernardino Mountains east of Los Angeles. The students were Class I paraglider pilots—and pals of Norma Jean's. All were nervous to take on the more turbulent air that accompanies thermals and, even more daunting, Southern California's heavy air traffic.

Her friend Inci waited for all the others to launch. A case of the jitters had overtaken her, and she worried about her ability to concentrate.

Norma Jean smiled and put a hand on her shoulder. This sort of thing had sometimes happened during her guiding days on Denali. Climbers would get overwhelmed by the enormity of the peak or the difficulty of the route. Then, as now, she would help them break down the task into familiar pieces.

"I need you to zero in on inflating the canopy, and nothing else. Got it? Once that's done, you'll take on the launch and only the launch. Once you're in the air, you can think thermals. Yes?"

Norma Jean hugged her and felt her nod in agreement.

She stepped back, and added: "I'll be on the radio with you."

Inci's face relaxed and she readied herself for the launch.

Norma Jean and another instructor watched as she maneuvered to the closest thermal. They talked her through the first five turns in the rising air, reminded her to feel the current and pay attention to her variometer, the instrument that measured vertical speed. Inci continued to circle upward, now unaided by the radio and even surpassed more experienced pilots.

"She's got this," Norma Jean said. Feel-good goosebumps tickled her scalp.

With all six aloft and two already on their way to the landing zone, it was finally her turn. Had she missed the day's prime conditions? She placed her usual prayer to the wind gods. Today of all days, she needed to soar with her students.

"I'm the *instructor*," she reminded the gods as she sprinted to the edge. "Let me join them."

Her canopy burst into the air and towed her heavenward.

She spotted her good friend Kari, at the top of the column of paragliders. Norma Jean began circling and climbing, easing her way upward for forty-five minutes. She reached 4,000 feet and sailed around Kari. The two exchanged a laugh, continuing their flights until the sun began to set and the valley below dimmed. She longed for more daylight.

Taking their time, they spiraled down to the landing zone and joined the group. Norma Jean never tired of the post-flight bliss, the excitement, and the back and forth among the pilots. Everyone shared tales of flying with hawks and close calls with hang gliders. Margaret described how she recovered from a spin.

The group piled into the van for the ride to the hotel.

Someone asked Norma Jean about the most unusual things she had learned in her time as an instructor. She thought for a moment.

"I never expected to be able to sprint backward, going downhill."

The others laughed.

"Didn't realize I could talk to famous people without getting starstruck."

Nods of recognition. Everyone there knew people in the movie industry, and Norma Jean counted several Lucas Studios employees as former students. She was close with bestselling author Richard Bach and his best friend, attorney Peter Buck. The connection would soon come in handy.

As the van motored along through the dark, she remembered how it had felt to move to California three years before and start anew. From the first day, she had engulfed herself in the Chandelle school and the near-perfect conditions for paragliding in Marin County. The time apart granted emotional distance between her and Clark, ending their marriage but preserving their friendship. They stayed in touch through letters and calls. She kept up with other Alaska friends, too. Hearing the details of their alpine adventures had made her worry that she was going soft. There was nothing like braving a mountain storm—fighting against gravity and ice, fear and unimaginable cold—to keep a person in top shape.

She had traveled home to visit Mother and Dad and spend another summer guiding at the Kachemak Bay Wilderness Lodge. Alaska still tugged at her and the yearning lingered even after she returned to California. Playing and replaying in her mind was John Muir's timeless statement about the mountains calling. She began to doubt whether she could dwell any longer in these mild green hills, idyllic as they were.

Then two things happened that made her rethink a return to the 49th state. Mother and Dad sold their house in Palmer and moved to Grants Pass, Oregon. And worse, oh, so much worse, an old friend betrayed her in the most public and humiliating manner.

• • •

Eight years before Norma Jean's 1990 solo summit of Denali, a woman named Miri Ercolani had claimed to reach the top by herself. She was a 54-year-old Italian doctor who landed on the

Kahiltna Glacier on July 3, 1982, and told people she had summited on July 21. Six days later, pilot Lowell Thomas, Jr. picked her up at Base Camp and flew her back to Talkeetna. He did not believe she had truly summited, and she offered no proof. Nonetheless, her name was recorded by the National Park Service as the first woman to complete a solo summit of the mountain.

Well aware of Ercolani's claim and its place in the records, Norma Jean had always qualified her own achievement: She was the first woman to make a *documented* solo summit of Denali. Norma Jean had the photos she had taken from the summit and a pair of climbers as witnesses.

Her old friend, a well-known author with whom she had climbed, kayaked, camped, and enjoyed long conversations, wrote that Norma Jean had tried to usurp Ercolani's title. In a book about Denali, he painted her as an attention-seeker. He described her as "garrulous" and eager to feed a "voracious Alaska press with a posed cover photo on Alaska magazine." Conversely, he called Ercolani "venerable" and repeated her implication that Norma Jean was simply out for publicity.

Not only was Norma Jean embarrassed by the portrayal, she also felt destabilized. If someone she had counted as a friend and had spent weeks with on group outings disdained her this much, were there others? Did his words reframe the way her peers saw her?

She consulted attorney Peter Buck about suing for libel.

"There is a case here," he said.

Her heart beat faster, and she began feeling lightheaded.

He met her gaze and steepled his fingers. "But, if we're going to do this, you need to be prepared."

"For? ..."

"For spending years of your life on how this affected you. Years of your life in the same, unhappy mindset."

Her heart tapered back to its normal rate, and her lightheadedness disappeared. She felt disappointed but also relieved. "It doesn't sound worth it."

"I don't think so, either," he said. "But it's your call."

That was it, then. She wouldn't sue, and she wouldn't move back home. The mountains were calling, but perhaps not that big one in Alaska.

With time and perspective, Norma Jean came to see her stretch in Marin as a segue between her early life and a newer, even richer version that came after.

In 1993, she took a ski trip to Palisades Tahoe (then known as Squaw Valley) in the Olympic Valley, two hundred miles northeast of Point Reyes. She lost herself in slaloming the resort's upper mountain, filled with peace. An alpine view of Lake Tahoe reminded her of the slopes at Alyeska, with Turnagain Arm in the distance. If she moved here, she could ski all winter—backcountry, cross country, and downhill—rock climb and bike in the summer—even kayak in Lake Tahoe. She could continue paragliding. With Mother and Dad only a six-hour drive away, the area had all the ingredients of home. She would make it so.

Before returning to Marin County, she began formulating a plan to move. She would miss her friends at Chandelle, but this simply felt right. It wasn't something she could explain, just plain old intuition making the call, sort of like the sensation she got before catching a thermal. She smiled, thinking of the question she always asked her students before they launched.

"Ready to fly?"

Yes, she was.

EPILOGUE
# Permanent Landing

**1993-Present**

Norma Jean took a sales job at a bike and ski shop in the town of Truckee not far from the Palisades Tahoe Resort and Olympic Valley (both known as Squaw Valley at the time). She moved there in the fall of 1993, yet it took a couple of months before she was fully settled. Working in the shop during the week, she made the four-hour drive back to Marin County on weekends to ensure her paragliding students could finish out their full courses at Chandelle. For the first three summers after the move, she returned to her guiding job at the Kachemak Bay Wilderness Lodge.

Truckee had a small-town feel, like Palmer, but it was geared toward outdoor recreation rather than farming. She rented a two-hundred-square-foot cabin on Donner Lake, about three miles from the shop. The cabin sat behind a regular house, but it was heated by woodstove, and her bedroom in the loft was accessible only by ladder. The cabin's rusticity felt charming at first, and fitting for an outdoorswoman, but in the winter, it was cold and uncomfortable. Still, it was her own space, and she relished it.

She made friends with coworkers at Truckee Ski Works as well as people she met on the trails, slopes, and in the backcountry. After about a year, she began dating the shop's ski tuner, a likeminded soul named Dave Bowers who also craved the mountains. Dave, who was a property manager for private homes and rental units during the day, worked nights at the shop to get employee discounts on gear and lift tickets. Before they met, he had studied forestry at the College of the Redwoods and worked as a helicopter ski guide in Nevada's Ruby Mountains. He also had an array of practical skills that had impressed Norma Jean: welding, auto mechanics, electrician work, and carpentry. He was a go-getter with a creative spirit, and she was soon smitten.

After deciding he was done with real estate, Dave joined a construction company and continued refining his carpentry craft. They combined households and then married in 1997. Norma Jean continued on at the shop while figuring out her next career move. Eventually she decided to pursue massage therapy. (It was a skill she was well acquainted with. As a teenager, she had taught herself reflexology to help ease her father's painful feet and hand after his workplace accident.)

In 2004, she received her certification and began working full time. Her new calling allowed her to tap into her experience as a mountaineer, paraglider, kayaker, and skier and gave her special insight into the needs of her outdoorsy clients. With hands made strong by years of climbing, she could wrest the knots out of the tightest muscles.

Through the early 2000s, she helped guide decisions about her aging parents' care. Her mother passed away in 2005, and her father eight months later, in 2006.

Though Norma Jean is proud of her successful solo summit of Denali and the experiences that led up to it, she has nothing else to prove as a mountaineer. In her words:

"The solo gave me a lot of confidence in myself, but still, life throws so many crazy angles at you, like losing your parents. Nobody gives you a guidebook on that. Trying to make sense of that process: Am I making good decisions with my parents? Those are the big, important things in life, and so I think the solo just kind of put it in perspective for me, that it's bigger out there. It's more important than just one mountain. There are bigger things in life."

She recently cut back her massage therapy schedule and often heads on hiking or cross-country ski trips with a group of women friends. They call themselves Team M (for mellow), though their interpretation of the word is surely more intense than most people's. They have racked up a number of memorable, never-again experiences over the years.

Dave still works full time as a home builder, specializing in custom woodworking. He spent ten years transforming a tiny, rundown "science project of a house" in the Olympic Valley into their forever home. The two ski, climb, and trek together in California, Canada, Alaska, and around the world. All just for fun. Norma Jean prizes her family ties, her friendships, her place in her community, and her marriage most of all. She said:

"I think the thing that's the very most important is my husband Dave and our life that we've created together. Which is a life full of adventure without me having to go solo on a big, scary mountain. We have a life full of adventure and full of love. And I'm most grateful for him. That is truly the most important thing."

## AFTERWORD
# How This Book Came to be

Norma Jean was at home in Olympic Valley, California in July 2022 when her phone rang. On the line was Bryan Burns, a friend she hadn't talked with in ages. He had news. A writer named Chris Lundgren—the wife of a guy he'd skied with back in high school—would like to interview her about her 1990 solo climb of Denali. And she wanted to write a book.

(And, by the way, Norma Jean had climbed Denali?! Alone?! He had no idea!)

Yes, it was true, and yes, Bryan could share her phone number with this writer. Privately, she figured she could talk Chris out of it. Who would want to read about her expedition after all this time?

"How did she find out about me?" Norma Jean asked.

"Well, that's the funny part. She was at some restaurant in Anchorage, and there were pictures of you on the wall."

• • •

Two months earlier my husband Carl and I were eating in the Arctic Roadrunner, an old-timey burger joint that's been around since the mid-1960s. Plastering the walls were pictures of notable locals, along with a short description of each and a blurb about how long they had been a customer at the restaurant. A framed collage of an Alaska magazine article from November 1990 hung above our booth. The cover photo, taken inside a studio, showed a beautiful, blonde mountaineer suspended midair on a rope.

She wore colorful climbing gear and looked at ease. The name "Norma Jean Saunders" floated underneath her backpack. A banner across the top of the magazine said, "FIRST WOMAN TO SOLO MCKINLEY?"

The display contained action shots of Norma Jean on the mountain and snippets from the article. One quote of hers stood out to me, suggesting that even though she was an adventurer, she was unafraid to be vulnerable—and probably possessed a sense of humor.

"At the summit, I cried. The altitude does funny things, makes you sentimental and blubbery."

She sounded relatable, someone whose book I'd like to read. A cursory Amazon search on my phone turned up nothing, nor did a more extensive hunt at the library. Besides the Alaska magazine feature, all that turned up were a couple of articles in the archives of the Anchorage Daily News.

Nobody had published a book about Norma Jean Saunders? As a writer, I sensed an opportunity.

Further digging revealed that her last name had changed from Saunders to Bowers at some point and that she lived around the Lake Tahoe area of California. Finding a current phone number or email proved futile.

Carl was Facebook friends with an old ski pal who now lived in the same area as Norma Jean. He messaged Bryan, and soon the connection was made.

• • •

"So that's how you found me?" Norma Jean joked the first time we talked. "Up on some wall?"

We had a good laugh, and it was the start of a two-year-long conversation about her journey from aspiring teenage mountaineer to the first woman to make a documented solo summit of Denali. Through a score of phone interviews, dozens of emails, countless texts, and an afternoon of talking in person, she relayed her story. She entrusted me with original photographs, slides, documents, and even the Denali map she'd carried in her backpack on her expeditions. She provided contact information for her climbing contemporaries and called the National Park Service in Talkeetna when she needed to fact-check herself.

Norma Jean was willing to answer anything, even the same question asked different ways. Grant Sims, the editor of Alaska magazine when her cover story was published, wrote: "We found her a delight. Whether for interviews, photos, studio sittings, prying questions or clarifications, Norma Jean made it easy, with a smile."

With the care and patience of a natural-born teacher, she demystified mountain climbing for me. But even as I immersed myself in Norma Jean's world, I never fully understood her. One day I asked if she ever got used to crevasses. Was there a point at which they just faded into the scenery and became unscary?

"Never," she said. "Because each time I've been on Denali, somebody has fallen to their death in a crevasse."

There were other horrors to consider: slipping on an icy slope, frostbite, hypothermia, altitude sickness. She came face to face with all of them, but her desire to climb was always bigger than her fears. So she became proficient in all aspects of mountaineering and then just kept adding to her skillset.

After Norma Jean completed her solo summit in 1990, she made some radical changes. Yet every succeeding part of her life has been informed by the confidence she gained during the decade-plus she spent on and around Denali.

Throughout the time we collaborated, I came across further evidence of her achievements: a few more archived newspaper stories about her successful solo in 1990, notices of public presentations she was scheduled to give at the time, articles in national paragliding magazines from the early 1990s, and a 2016 feature story in a Lake Tahoe-area 'zine. But given her exceptional tale, these are all just faint scratches on the historical record. I hope this book leaves an indelible mark.

Norma Jean has never considered herself anything more than ordinary, but I think this is what makes her story so extraordinary.

A funny little plaque under the Arctic Roadrunner display puts it in context:

"Norma Jean, First Woman to Solo Mt. McKinley's 20,320 ft, June 11, 1990. Arctic Roadrunner Customer Since 1968."

## APPENDIX 1
# Norma Jean's 1990 Denali Packing List

8-foot ladder
Wands
Sled, including duffel bag, bungee
Accessory straps
6 carabiners
Koflach boots
4 pr. socks
2 pr. liner socks
Vapor barrier socks
Polarguard booties
Lt. wt. polypro top and bottoms
Hvy. wt. polypro top and bottoms
Pile jacket (fleece)
Gortex jacket
Down parka
Pile hat
Scarf
Sleeping pads
Sleeping bag
Tent
Stove
Pot, cup, spoon
2 water bottles
Swiss Army Knife
Backpack and little pouch

2 polypro liner gloves
Hvy. wt. gloves (ski gloves)
Summit mittens
Pile pants
Gortex pants
Harness
Shovel
Gaiters and overboots
Foot fang crampons
Mountaineering skis and ski skins
Ski poles
Ice axe
2 ice screws
Deadmen (anchor for tent)
Rope, 40 feet
Garbage bags
Jumars
Stuff sacks
Food, 18 days
Fuel
Bic lighters

REPAIR KIT:
    Allen wrench
    Screwdriver
    Ski binding repair parts
    Foot fang repair parts
    Needless, material,
    Safety pins, gray duct tape
    Baling wire

TOILETRIES
    Sm. brush
    Toothbrush, paste
    Tweezers
    Floss

Sunscreen, lip balm
Sm. Mirror

FIRST AID KIT
Aspirin, moleskin
Athletic tape, Band Aids
Ace bandage, burn ointment
Diamox, Decatron
Emprin, Compazine
Imodium, Betadine cream

# APPENDIX 2
# Recognition from the Alaska State Legislature

"THE SEAL OF THE STATE OF ALASKA"
*HONORING*
*NORMA JEAN SAUNDERS*

"The members of the Sixteenth Alaska Legislature salute and congratulate Norma Jean Saunders for her courage and determination in completing her solo climb to the summit of Mount McKinley on June 11, 1990.

Currently a resident of the Matanuska-Susitna Borough in Palmer, Norma Jean is an outgoing, positive and respected individual. She moved to Alaska with her parents, Norman and Jean Marsh, and her brothers James and William, in the early 1960s. She enjoyed an active childhood and learned to appreciate the unique lure and challenges of the Alaskan outdoors.

A 1978 graduate of Palmer High School, Norma Jean still resides and works with her husband, Clark, in the Valley. Together, they have developed their business, Raven Adventures, and are professed by many to be two of the most outstanding parasailing instructors in the country.

The trek up North America's highest peak is a treacherous one marred with unpredictable and often severe conditions that very few individuals are able to withstand alone. Norma Jean's accomplishment holds special meaning in the minds of many fellow Alaskans who praise her ability to conquer Mt. McKinley. The State of Alaska is proud to recognize the efforts of Norma Jean Saunders."

# HISTORICAL NOTES

**CHAPTER 1 HISTORICAL NOTE**
**Denali's Big Year**

The year 2015 was a big one for The Tall One. First, the mountain's traditional name, Denali, was restored. Derived from a Koyukon Athabaskan word (deenaalee, which translates to "the tall one"), the name was made official on August 28 of that year. People had been calling it Mt. McKinley since 1917, despite the fact that its namesake, President William McKinley of Ohio, had no known connection to Alaska or the mountain, nor had he ever visited the territory. Secretary of the Interior Sally Jewell (under President Barack Obama) used her authority to make the change, which State officials had been trying to do for four decades.

Also in 2015, the summit elevation was resurveyed and determined to be 20,310 feet. This was slightly lower than the previously accepted elevation of 20,320 feet, which had been established in 1953 through a photogrammetric survey. The June 2015 survey expedition used GPS and other modern methods to verify the new elevation.

**CHAPTER 5 HISTORICAL NOTE**
**Denali Damsels**

In 1970, the six-member Denali Damsels became the first all-women's team to summit Denali. It consisted of graduate student Arlene Blum (25), chemistry teacher Dana Smith Isherwood (34), expedition leader and anesthesiologist Grace Hoeman (48), physicist, pilot, and airplane mechanic Margaret Young (37), geology student and New Zealander Margaret Clark (35), and Australian Faye Kerr (39), trained as a teacher, but who instead took various jobs to support her climbing.

On June 21 of that year, pilot Don Sheldon flew the Damsels into Kahiltna Base Camp to begin their journey. All started with seventy-pound packs, which they lightened along the way as they climbed expedition style.

Blum had broken her leg six months earlier but recovered sufficiently for the climb. She found herself playing peacekeeper between the combative Hoeman and Smith Isherwood. The rest of the team avoided Hoeman when possible to keep from triggering her ire.

Hoeman began showing symptoms of altitude sickness early in the expedition. She complained of headaches and grew more argumentative. Above 18,000 feet, she became clumsy, and Smith Isherwood helped her climb the last few steps to the summit.

The Damsels celebrated at the summit on July 6, 1970, with chocolate fudge, smoked oysters, and dried apricots. They took pictures but didn't tarry. Blum assumed the role of leader while Hoeman was unwell.

The team rallied together to coordinate and take on Hoeman's rescue during the descent. This entailed overnighting at 18,200-foot Denali Pass. In the morning, Hoeman was able to walk and downclimb with assistance. The team finished the descent safely.

Blum went on to lead the first American team (which was also all female) up Nepal's Annapurna I in 1978. Her book about the experience, *Annapurna: A Woman's Place,* was published in 1980 and reissued twenty years later.

Three chapters of her 2005 book, *Breaking Trail: A Climbing Life,* detail the Denali Damsels' successful summit.

On the event's fiftieth anniversary, the National Park Service posted a tribute on its blog. An excerpt puts the achievement in perspective:

"While Barbara Washburn [the first woman to climb Denali] set the bar by standing on the summit, the Denali Damsels planned and executed the entire expedition, thus raising the bar for the next generations. Not only that, the Denali Damsels performed a heroic self-rescue that goes beyond what most people would be capable of. ... The team completed the descent in style and without further mishaps, all while singing at the top of their lungs, according to Blum's account."

## CHAPTER 8 HISTORICAL NOTE
### Barbara Washburn, the First Woman to Climb Denali

Preceding Norma Jean's solo summit by forty-three years, Barbara Washburn was the first female climber to attempt Denali *and* the first female climber to reach the top. Barbara, her husband, cartographer Bradford Washburn, and a team of scientists proceeded up the Muldrow Glacier in the spring of 1947. The Muldrow was the most common route to the summit, though simply climbing the mountain at all was still uncommon. They summited on June sixth.

Brad was director of the Boston Museum of Science and a well-known mountain explorer, photographer, and cartographer. He collected geographic information on Denali. (And four years later, he pioneered the West Buttress route.) Other team members studied cosmic rays, weather patterns, and geology.

The Washburns had left their three children, ages nine months to six years, in the care of a paid nurse with both sets of grandparents nearby. Barbara felt torn, and getting back to them safely was her driving force during the expedition.

By 1947, she was a skilled mountaineer, which was almost unheard of for a woman in those days. She had made first ascents of Mt. Bertha in the southeast part of Alaska in 1940 and Mt. Hayes north of Fairbanks in 1941 with Brad and his teams. (World War II prohibited any missions they might have undertaken between 1941 and 1947.) When not climbing, Barbara was a housewife and stay-at-home mother in Boston. Unlike Norma Jean, who was in top shape for her expeditions, Barbara could not prioritize physical training. She joked that she got into shape by pushing a baby carriage. Fittingly, she used her homemaking skills to design dehydrated meals for herself and her teams before the Denali trip.

Mountaineering clothes mostly came from military surplus in the 1940s and were nonexistent for women. Photos of Barbara show her engulfed in ill-fitting men's wool pants and a down parka with the sleeves rolled up.

Barbara's exploits are captured well in her book, *The Accidental Adventurer: Memoirs of the First Woman to Climb Mt. McKinley*, which she coauthored with journalist Lew Freedman. The Denali expedition in which she took part is detailed in an eighteen-minute documentary, called "Operation White Tower." It was released in theaters in 1948 and is now on YouTube.

Barbara Washburn went on to become an award-winning remedial reading teacher for twenty years. She also received an honorary doctorate from the University of Alaska in 1995 for the cartography work she performed on the 1947 Denali expedition. She received many joint awards and honors with Bradford as well.

## CHAPTER 10 HISTORICAL NOTE
### Peter Hackett and Medical Camp

Peter Hackett, M.D., is a mountaineer and an internationally recognized authority on high-altitude medicine and physiology.

In 1982, he established a medical research camp at the 14,200-foot basin—a place that was commonly used as a stopover point for climbers. The area was already known as Camp 3 and 14 Camp, but because of Hackett's work with the Denali Medical Research Project, it was also nicknamed Medical Camp.

There, from May 1 to July 1 through most of the 1980s, he studied (and provided aid to) climbers suffering from hypothermia, frostbite, and altitude-related illnesses. Studies conducted by Hackett's Denali Medical Research Project contributed to the worldwide understanding of these issues. Based on his findings, the practice of taking on high elevations in stages is now standard.

From his base in Medical Camp, Hackett joined helicopter rescues on the mountain's upper reaches. This way he could provide medical care as quickly as possible.

The idea for Medical Camp came about when Hackett and Denali Park Ranger Bob Gerhard discussed ways to reduce medical emergencies on the mountain. Hackett had an ongoing interest in studying altitude sickness that started with his own teammates' experiences on 29,032-foot Mt. Everest. He conducted one of the first studies on the drug Diamox to prevent and treat mountain sickness in 1975, and the success of the study convinced him to devote himself to high-altitude medicine.

He cooperated with many others to make Denali's Medical Camp a reality. Dr Bill Mills, an orthopedic surgeon and frostbite expert in Anchorage had recently received an appropriation from the Alaska Legislature to research cold-related injuries. Mills provided the funding and Hackett provided the expertise and the technology.

In 1981, Hackett and others climbed and studied Denali, deciding that the basin at 14,200 feet was the right site for the camp. It was close enough to the upper reaches of the mountain and large enough to allow helicopter landings.

The U.S. Army flew in 7,000 pounds of equipment that first summer. It included two WeatherPort canvas structures and a solar-powered energy system that would allow Hackett and his team to run their medical equipment.

"Over the years we had everything from echocardiography, electroencephalography, to blood gas analyzers," he said in an interview in 2000. "Lots of different kinds of medical equipment and even air compressors when we were experimenting with hyperbaric chambers."

Denali climbers were interested in the group's research. Many teams stopped by to visit with the doctors and physiologists and also to have their oxygen levels tested.

"I think that's how we prevented a lot of problems, just through education and screening," Hackett said. "We could pick up pulmonary edema in fifteen seconds with these little pulse oximeters. And then we would tell the people to stay there and rest or go down before going any higher. I'm sure we saved a lot of deaths and rescues that way."

The Park Service set up camp alongside Hackett's group. Mountaineering rangers would stay in camp for an extended time and become acclimated at 14,000 feet. This meant they could access the upper mountain within just a few hours and provide aid where needed. The Park Service continued to maintain an outpost there after Hackett's group left.

Medical Camp was a difficult place to conduct research.

"At times we had to forget about any kind of research and just concentrate on survival: digging ourselves out, keeping the tents unburied or damaged," Hackett said in 2000. During the more intense storms, the team moved into the WeatherPort structures that were normally just their workspace and kitchen.

Hackett and his team were at the 14,200-foot site during climbing season between 1982 and 1989. By late in the decade, it had become harder to find subjects for their studies on altitude sickness.

"One reason was that we had done a good job of warning the public about the dangers of altitude climbing, doing a lot of preventive education, screening people for pulmonary edema so that the number of cases was going steadily down. Therefore we were running out of subjects. In a sense, we put ourselves out of business."

As so, it became harder to justify running the program to the group's funding agencies—the National Institutes of Health and the American Heart Association.

In 1990, the Army sent its helicopters to the Middle East as the Gulf Conflict ramped up. The Denali Medical Research Project team could not get its equipment onto Denali. Hackett received permission from the American Heart Association to transfer the project to Keystone Ski Resort in Colorado, which ranges from 9,280 feet at the base to a summit elevation of 12,408 feet. Hackett found many new subjects to study among the downhill skiers.

"Over spring break we saw about 15 cases of high-altitude pulmonary edema in a short period of time. That was a much better yield than Mt. McKinley," Hackett said. "And we didn't have survival situations."

Though the group departed Denali, the National Park Service mountaineering ranger outpost continues to carry on each climbing season. Fourteen Camp is still commonly called Medical Camp.

# AUTHOR'S NOTES

*Her Denali Solo: A Woman Alone on North America's Highest Peak* is recreated from Norma Jean's journals, other writings, photographs, memories, official records, newspaper and magazine articles, and interviews with her contemporaries. Because the events happened three to four decades before the writing of this book, some information we gathered seemed unclear or even contradictory. We have done our best—independently and as a team—to verify the information and tell Norma Jean's authentic story.

We used real names to the best of our ability, but in some cases last names or entire names were lost to history.

Norma Jean created a written account of some of her experiences, such as her Ruth Glacier expedition and climb of Mt. Dan Beard (and its aftermath), as well as her Women on Denali expedition. She also crafted an excellent magazine article about riding thermals in her paraglider. All of her writing was insightful and descriptive and it gave me a wealth of material from which to build the related chapters.

During her first solo attempt in 1986, Norma Jean fell and slid down a steep area called the Autobahn. Her sense of being helped to her feet by another person on that empty slope was real to her. Not wanting others to think she was delusional, she told very few people about the incident. Recently, though, she discovered that other adventurers have reported similar experiences with "third-man factor," or "third-man syndrome"—the sense that some beneficent soul was present during a life-threatening experience. Among them were world-renowned Italian climber Reinhold

Messner; British climber Joe Simpson (author of the book, *Touching the Void*); American polar explorer Ann Bancroft; and early twentieth century Anglo-Irish explorer Ernest Shackleton.

Mt. McKinley was the mountain's legal name during the period of Norma Jean's climbing career, but many Alaskans continued to call it by its traditional name, Denali. The name was officially changed in 2015. We have thus referred to it as Denali throughout the book.

Finally, a bit of cautionary advice from Norma Jean:

"I feel it is really important that we do not glamorize solo climbing. It is so extremely dangerous and most routes have been soloed now by men and women. I would so not want to encourage anyone else to climb Denali solo. I just hope we are not going to give people the idea that the only way they can find their limits and their personal knowledge is to put themselves in great danger. Lately I have encouraged other women to hike long distance on the Pacific Crest Trail or other high routes."

# BIBLIOGRAPHY AND SOURCES

**Books:**

*Accidents in North American Mountaineering*, published by the American Alpine Club, 1981, 1985, 1987, 1989, and 1991.

Coombs, Colby, with photographs by Washburn, Bradford, *Denali's West Buttress: A Climber's Guide to Mount McKinley's Classic Route*, Mountaineers Books, Seattle WA, 1997. This book was my bible for over two years.

Puryear, Joseph, *Alaska Climbing*, Super Topo Guidebooks, c. 2006

Hill, Pete, and Johnston, Stuart, *The Mountain Skills Training Handbook*, David & Charles Publishing, 2001

Richard, Sukey, Orr, Donna, and Lindholm, Claudia, eds *The NOLS Cookery: Experience the Art of Outdoor Cooking … A Publication of The National Outdoor Leadership School* and Stackpole Books, 1988 (updated 1991)

Blum, Arlene, *Breaking Trail: A Climbing Life*, Mariners Books, 2007

Freedman, Lew, *Denali Ranger: A Life of Drama and Adventure on America's Tallest Peak* (about Roger Robinson), Epicenter Press, 2017

Thomas, Lowell Jr. and Freedman, Lew., *Lowell Thomas Jr., Flight to Adventure: Alaska and Beyond*, p. 238 (re: Norma Jean and Miri Ercolani), Alaska Northwest Books, 2013

Washburn, Barbara, and Freedman, Lew, *The Accidental Adventurer: Memoirs of the First Woman to Climb Mt. McKinley*, Epicenter Press, 2001

Tejas, Vern, and Freedman, Lew, *Seventy Summits: Life in the Mountains*, Blue River Press, 2017

Davidson, Art, *Minus 148 Degrees: First Winter Ascent of Mt. McKinley*, W.W. Norton, 1969

**Internet:**

Project Jukebox, Digital Branch of the University of Alaska Fairbanks Oral History Program. The website provides audio and video recordings of history-making Alaskans, along with supporting materials. There is an entire section on Denali Mountaineering. I listened to audio tapes of Colby Coombs, Art Davidson, Doug Geeting, Peter Hackett, Dave Johnston, Jim Okonek, Barbara Washburn, and Bradford Washburn. See jukebox.uaf.edu/denali

National Park Service website, to confirm details on various aspects of Denali for the body of the book and several sidebar segments throughout the book. See nps.gov/denali

"How to Climb Denali: Strategies and Advice from Steve House and Mark Postle," a two-hour presentation through the Uphill Athlete channel on YouTube. The presentation was filmed for hopeful climbers during Covid, May 7, 2020. See uphillathlete.com

American Alpine Institute website provides an excellent description of climbing the West Buttress route along with photos, maps, and videos. See alpineinstitute.com

Mountain Trip Alaska guiding service's website also provides an excellent description of climbing the West Buttress route along with photos, maps, and videos. See summitdenali.com/denali-west-buttress

Climbing the Seven Summits YouTube channel offers excellent advice on climbing Denali. See climbingthesevensummits.com

**Magazine and Newspaper Articles:**

Freedman, Lew, *Alaska: The Magazine of Life on the Last Frontier*, November 1990, vol. 56, no. 11, p. 36, "Norma Jean Saunders, At Last Alone at the Top"

**Anchorage Daily News:**
Climbing, Special Sports Section on Mountaineering in Alaska, July 14, 1991, p. 26, "Tempting Fate Comes with Territory."
Freedman, Lew, "Mt. McKinley: Alone at the Top Norma Jean Stands," June 24, 1990, p. D1
Medred, Craig, "Alone on McKinley", June 7, 1986, p. A1
Porco, Peter, *We Alaskans Magazine* (published by Anchorage Daily News), "First Impressions: The Summit Isn't Everything," June 29, 1986, p. 5
Hunter, Don, "Climbers' Bodies Recovered," Friday, June 6, 1980, p. C1

**Anchorage Times:**
Jacques Picard, "Woman Hits McKinley Summit Solo" June 12, 1990, p. A-1
Bill Kelder, "Woman Returns Home Exhausted After Solo Ascent of Denali" June 13, 1990, p. A-3
"First Woman on McKinley Credits Husband's Support," June 29, 1990, p. D-1 by staff

**Other Periodicals:**
Bachelor, Blane, "The Remarkable Tale of Norma Jean Bowers," *Roots Rated online 'zine*, July 19, 2016
Thompson, Lisa, November 4, 1994, "Norma Jean Marsh: Solo Climb to the Summit, p. 9, *College of Marin Echo Times*.
Moir, Allison "Stressbusters: The Icarus Complex: The Irresistible Sport of Paragliding," September 26, 1994, *Forbes, FYI, a Supplement to Forbes Magazine*, p. 36

Stockwell, Claudia, , "Women with Wings", *Paragliding: The Magazine. Vol. 3, no. 2, 1992, p.10*

Marsh, Norma Jean, , "Maiden Voyages in Thermals," *Paragliding: The Magazine*, July/August 1994, vol. 5, #4, p.36.

Bach, Richard, "Under the Rainbow: A Discovery of Paragliding", p. 4, *Paragliding: The Magazine, Special New Pilots Edition* 1994 (no volume/number)

**Hands-On:**

Talkeetna Air Taxi flightseeing tour around Denali on May 27, 2024. At my request, pilot Andy Young made sure I got an eyeful of Denali's West Buttress route as he described it in detail.

# ABOUT THE AUTHOR

Chris Lundgren is the author of three other books: *Accidental Adventures: Alaska—True Tales of Ordinary People Facing Danger in the Wilderness* (Lyons Press, 2020); *Legendary Locals of Chugiak-Eagle River* (Arcadia Publishing, 2014); and the *Runner's World Guide to Running and Pregnancy* (Rodale Books, 2003). She has lived in Eagle River, Alaska, with her family since 1997. When not writing, she enjoys hiking, running, cross-country skiing, kayaking, and swimming.

(Top) The house that Norma Jean grew up in still sits on a ridge above the Alaska State Fairgrounds in Palmer. The chalet was brought over from Switzerland and assembled from labeled parts. When Norma Jean lived there in the 1970s, the home had a concrete bomb shelter.

(Left) Backcountry climbing and skiing at Hatcher Pass in the late 1980s.

Sharpening her ice-climbing skills on the Matanuska Glacier on a warm day in 1987.

Leaping across a crevasse on the Matanuska Glacier in 1987. Despite appearances, Norma Jean always maintained a healthy fear of crevasses.

Kahiltna Base Camp with Denali's summit in the background. The West Buttress route winds its way around the left side of the rocky peak in the foreground.

The one-person, bicycle-touring tent that Norma Jean used on her 1986 solo attempt, pictured here at Kahiltna Base Camp. The tent was lightweight and compact but not practical for Denali, as it was quickly buried under heavy snowfalls. The fabric repelled moisture but didn't breathe. Norma Jean found it claustrophobic and regretted taking it.

Norma Jean at 11,000 feet looking up toward Windy Corner during the first solo attempt in 1986. Glacier glasses and zinc oxide protect her eyes, nose, and lips from the sun. Warmer temperatures allow her to substitute thick long johns for pants.

Norma Jean dries out gear at High Camp at 17,200 feet during her 1986 solo attempt. As promised to a friend and benefactor, she poses with a can of SPAM.

With parents, Jean and Norman Marsh at Kahiltna Base Camp in summer 1986.

Camp at 14,200 feet on a June day during the 1990 solo climb. Norma Jean's tent was dome style—a big improvement from the low-slung tent she used in 1986—but was also made of unbreathable fabric and required frequent clearing during snowstorms. Note how the snow-block walls stand higher than the tent's apex to protect it from wind. The group of wands in the foreground bear the Raven Adventures logo.

Another day at 14 Camp during Norma Jean's 1990 solo expedition.

Washing up at 14 Camp during her 1990 solo expedition. Reaching 14,200 feet was a milestone in the climb. She made a ritual out of bathing here—a washcloth scrub-down inside the tent walls followed by a light shampoo outside. Her hair froze before slowly drying out.

A wind-bent wand let Norma Jean know she had reached the top in June 1990.

(Top) Looking past her boots and crampons to the expansive view from the summit in June 1990.

(Right) Pausing at 14 Camp on the 1990 descent.

(Top) A climber Norma Jean didn't know sent her this photo from her descent in June 1990. It was taken at approximately 8,000 feet as she passed the man's campsite. Note the deteriorating weather and Norma Jean's posture. She felt fatigued and uncertain where she would be when the storm hit.

(Left) The certificate from the Alaska State Legislature recognizing Norma Jean for her successful solo summit in June 1990.

*Alaska* magazine's November 1990 cover featuring Norma Jean's successful solo summit.

In 1947, Barbara Washburn became the first woman to summit Denali. She and Norma Jean met in late 1990 in Anchorage.

Though Norma Jean was hired to teach paragliding at Chandelle San Francisco Sky School, she also learned to hang glide. Here she is in 1994 on the same beginner hill from which her paragliding students made their first launches.

(Top) Norma Jean prepares a paragliding student—checking his harness and sharing last-minute reminders—before his launch from the beginner hill at Chandelle Sky School's Marin County flight grounds in 1995.

(Left) Skiing the backcountry at Hatcher Pass on a visit to Alaska, April 2023. Norma Jean and husband Dave Bowers return to the area every few years to visit friends and enjoy the spring snow.

Norma Jean and Dave Bowers visiting Alaska in April 2023.

Norma Jean and author Chris Lundgren meet in person for the first time in Eagle River, Alaska in April 2023.

Now in her sixties, Norma Jean still likes to play in the outdoors. She skis in the backcountry, mountain bikes, takes long-haul hikes, and rock climbs. She recently learned to swim and maintains a regular workout in Lake Tahoe through the summers. Here she takes part in a climb not far from her home in Olympic Valley, California in 2024.

Norma Jean and Dave Bowers rock climbing in Olympic Valley, California in 2024.

www.ingramcontent.com/pod-product-compliance
Lightning Source LLC
Chambersburg PA
CBHW011550070526
44585CB00023B/2527